**<u>The True Story</u> (

Russia 1918. A ba
the summer in the Urals to escape the miseries of
the Revolution, is cut off behind the lines and
eventually forced to beg and steal for their
survival as the harsh winter approaches.

American newspaper editor, Riley Allen,
working for the Red Cross as a press officer,
hears about the children and heads a team to
rescue them. Since they cannot go west back to
Petrograd, he takes them east across Siberia to
Vladivostok, but when the Japanese capture the
town he is forced to think again. He hires a small
Japanese freighter, fits it out to accommodate
900 people, and sails across the Pacific to San
Francisco, then through the Panama Canal, up to
New York and across the Atlantic to Europe.
After an epic and eventful journey of over two
years, the children cross the Finnish/Russian
border and are returned to their parents.

The children and teachers were obliged to keep
their story a secret throughout their lives since
the communist regime in the USSR would have
penalised them severely for having been to the
US.

The Long Way Home

Chapter 1

A volley of gunfire rattles the windows making me jump and dive for the floor with everyone else.

"That was close," whispers Grigori, beside me. "Are they going to come and shoot us too?" There is a tremor in his voice and he looks up at me for reassurance which I cannot give. I'm scared too.

No-one else speaks but I can hear their quick nervous breathing around me.

There's been gunfire most of the morning but that was further away down the hill in the village. We have been confined to the hotel all day and now I'm getting restless. I want to move, do something, not just crouch here like a frightened rabbit.

What are the soldiers doing here in the hotel grounds? Do they know we are here? Grigori might be right. Perhaps we *are* next.

The dust on the dry wooden floor catches in my throat and I struggle to try and suppress the cough but fail.

"You're nearest to the window, Nikolai, why don't you look and tell us what's happening?" It's Ivan and his tone is teasing with a hint of malice. Ignore him, I tell myself. I'm not afraid of him, as he would like. But he irritates me like a pebble in my shoe.

My curiosity is aroused but I hesitate a moment so it doesn't look as though I'm obeying Ivan's suggestion. Then I begin to struggle to my feet.

"No!" It's Grigori. I can see his wide scared eyes. He pulls at my sleeve trying to drag me back onto the floor. "You might get shot, Nikolai."

"He could do with a haircut," comes Ivan's voice. I hear laughter. There are always one or two who think his jokes are funny.

"Let go Grigori," I say, freeing myself from his grasp. "I have to see." I feel for the wooden windowsill above my head. Then I slowly pull myself up, eager to peer through the window and find out what is going on, yet afraid that the moment my head shows it will be blown to pieces. My heart thumps.

Someone outside shouts an order just as my eyes come level with the sill and I flinch but look out just the same.

Nausea hits me with a punch and my stomach heaves, trying to turn itself inside out. I swallow and take a deep breath to stop myself from throwing up. Then I look again.

A long line of bodies lies on the ground. One is on his back with his arms above his head as if in surrender. Two have crumpled in a heap and several are sprawled untidily against the wall where they were lined up. Dark blood spreads over the ground, running in rivulets between the cobbles.

I watch the firing squad turn and march out of the hotel forecourt, leaving the silent bloody bodies to cast long shadows as the sun sinks below the Ural Mountains.

I cannot take my eyes off them. I have never seen anyone dead before and I stare, expecting them to move, unable to accept the finality of it. A gust of wind lifts the hair on the one nearest to us and I hold my breath, looking for any sign of life. But he has not felt that breeze. How could he be alive when the face below the hair has gone?

I'm sure they are, or were, Red Russian soldiers although the ragged appearance of some show them to be partisans, young men, loyal to their beliefs, defeated – and now dead.

I am aware of movement behind me as others get to their feet but my head feels numb and if I move I'll be sick and they will all be disgusted and never let me forget it, especially Ivan.

I think about my father. He's dead too, just like these men. Another war but the same outcome.

At last I feel able to move and I turn and try to speak but my tongue is stuck to the roof of my dry mouth so I just hold up my hands and try to prevent them from looking out of the window.

Most of the children in the room are younger than me, except for Grigori and Ivan and a few others. Grigori is thirteen like me and Ivan says he's seventeen. But the young ones should not see this. None of us should see it.

"What's happened?" asks Grigori.

"An execution," I whisper. "A Czech firing squad. They have massacred some poor Red soldiers who were retreating anyway."

The door bursts open and one of our teachers, Miss Stepovich, comes in, white-faced. She scans the room, clutching at her long grey skirt with restless fingers.

"Is everyone all right?"

"Yes, Miss."

She tries to smile, to put us at our ease but only her mouth goes through the motions. Her eyes look dead. She stoops a little and opens her arms and, with a long sigh, embraces as many of the younger children as she can. "We are in the middle of another war," she says. "A war mostly between our own people, but we must try and be brave as your mothers and fathers would wish you to be."

The mention of parents reminds me about Anton and I look round for him. I'm meant to be looking after my younger brother but had forgotten him. I promised – no, I did *not* promise Mother. I had not wanted to come on this vacation as they called it, in the first place. I feel my jaw tighten as I remember the scene. She'd had no right to force me to come. Now that father is dead it is *my* job to help her. I should have refused to come. I *did* refuse to come but still, here I am, in the Ural mountains in a village which has become the front line of another war, when I should be at home with mother in Petrograd. Things are bad there too but at least we would be at home and together.

Anton had been crouching in a corner and when he catches my eye he slowly stands up and comes to me, his shoulders hunched. Now I feel his hand creep into mine and I resist the impulse to shake it off, even when I see Ivan's smirk. I look down at the small white face of my brother. No kid should have to go through this, especially following on from our father's death two months ago. Anton has taken it hard, but at least we are going home in September and this is July. We've been away two months and there are two more months to go.

Two days later we watch as the column of Czech soldiers on horseback move out of Koure in pursuit of the Red army to the west. They haven't bothered with us. They'd had more to think about than a couple of hundred children in a hotel on a retreat from the deprivation of the city.

Our teachers try to get things back to normal again in our hotel on the hill and we resume our activities, lessons in the mornings, free afternoons and songs and dancing in the evenings.

Singing? Ugh! I couldn't sing if my life depended on it. I hate this place too, with its stinking sulphurous smell. It's hard to believe that people actually came here to bathe in the smelly water.

The summer has been warm and sometimes we older children bathe in the river in the valley below the hotel, or go on hikes in the mountains. I like that. It is so different from our life in Petrograd. The war has begun to fade, except for the small garrison of Czech soldiers which remain in the village, but they don't bother anyone.

My spirits begin to rise as September draws near and the heat of the sun fades a little. I wonder more and more how things are in Petrograd. There have been food shortages there since the world war began back in 1914, and then had come the Revolution which had made things much worse. Here, I must admit, we are quite well fed. I worry about mother though. Is she hungry? Is she well? Does she still have her little job at the bakery bringing in a few roubles a week.

I wish I had not been in such a temper when we left her.

Chapter 2

"There's going to be a meeting," says Boris. "About going home."

"Good," I say. "I can't wait to get out of this smelly place." I know we should be grateful that our parents arranged this, but I can't see it that way at the moment.

"Where and when?"

Boris looks at me with his slightly absent-minded expression. "What? Oh, in the boys' dormitory after dinner."

"Dinner?" I say. "That's a grand name for it." He nods. I know Boris of old. He likes food, but there's been a scarcity of it in Petrograd for years. Before that, though, I remember some of the picnics we used to have in the holidays.

There is something wrong and we all know it. We should be going home. The weather is cooler and we only have our summer clothes. When we ask, the teachers avoid our questions. Do they think we are stupid? The food is running out too, we get smaller portions now. What happens when there is no more? We'll starve. We might as well starve at home with our families.

About fifty of us crowd into the dormitory that evening to decide who is going to talk to the teachers. We want to know the truth.

Ivan is here. He looks at me wide-eyed pretending to be astonished. "Not baby-sitting your brother today, Nikolai? No snivelling, whining appendage hanging onto your hand?"

I would agree if it wasn't Ivan who was saying it, but with him I feel defensive about my brother although I can't think of a smart retort.

"Shut up, Ivan," was the best I could muster. I push past him with more confidence than I feel. He's a lot bigger than me and he can't resist flicking my ear as I pass.

It stings, but I won't give him the satisfaction of acknowledging the pain. I look to the front and am surprised when a girl climbs onto a table and waves her hand for silence.

"My name's Tatiana," she says. "We've called this meeting to tell you what we propose to do. We all want to know when we are going home. They told us September and September is here but we are still here. We want to know the truth. We are intelligent young people and not young children . It is our right to know what is happening."

There are cheers and nods of agreement. I squint at her. She uses big words and isn't afraid to speak in front of the older ones but she can't be any older than me.

Ivan and his friends snigger and one of them says something which makes everyone nearby laugh. Oh, how he loves an appreciative audience. Tatiana glares at them briefly but then carries on.

"If no-one has any objections, five of us have volunteered to ask for a meeting with the teachers." She beckons to others to come forward and we all crane our necks to see. I don't think it matters who goes, so long as they get an answer.

It's over quickly. The five are going to propose a meeting with the teachers after church on Sunday.

The small church in Koure cannot accommodate all of us at once so we have been divided into four groups and go once a month. It is not our turn to go so when Sunday comes we wait for the others to return so that we can get an answer to our questions.

It is short and comes quickly.

We cannot go home.

We are cut off behind the battle lines of the Revolution. We are running out of food and winter is coming. The teachers do not know what to do. I knew I was right. If I'd had my way we wouldn't be here.

The day after the meeting Miss Stepovich speaks to us all as we finish our breakfast. She has a habit of smoothing her skirts when she stands up, and then lifting her head and standing tall to try to make the most of her height. She's not pretty but has a motherly face, I think. Her hair is always neatly tied in a chignon at the back of her neck.

"The revolution in our country has forced us to change our plans. We cannot pass through the fighting lines, it would be far too dangerous, but we cannot stay here either. This small village can't support a big group like this so we have decided to move further east to a bigger town down on the plain where the weather will not be as harsh as here in the mountains. We shall pack up what provisions we have and leave on Thursday. We'll give out paper and pencils for you to all write to your parents and tell them what's happening. At least some of the letters may get through.." She tried to finish with a smile. "Be brave and trust in God."

I'm not sure that God is anywhere near, especially as He's been banned since the Revolution. I know if I'd been banned I wouldn't stay around.

"Nikolai." It's Anton. He hardly speaks at all these days since father's death. "I want to go home."

I suddenly feel a lump in my throat and choke up. Oh how much I want that too. My anger at Mother has dissolved and now I just feel an awful guilt. I wallowed in anger when I thought we were going home soon but now our future is not clear. Who knows when we'll be home? I wish Mother and I had parted friends. I would give anything to relive that scene again.

Chapter 3

We had hardly been out of the hotel since the execution and now, as we leave it for the last time, we have to pass through the courtyard and over those same cobbles where, only a few weeks ago, all those men died so brutally.

I pull my jacket round me as we step out of the front door. A cool wind is blowing down from the mountains as a reminder that it is now October, summer is over, the leaves are changing, and we are not going home, but further away in the opposite direction.

I try to resist looking at the wall where those men died but my eyes swing round of their own accord. Of course the bodies have gone and someone has scrubbed the wall and the cobbles but you can't get rid of blood so easily. The dark stains are still there, as they should be. There has to be some reminder that those men once lived.

We each have a parcel of food, pretty much all that is left of our provisions. After that, who knows when we'll eat again. It's then that a thought bursts into my mind and with it spark of excitement. It is easier for two to find food than two hundred.

I find myself next to Tatiana as we walk in a long line down the hill and through the village. She's taller than me and holds herself very erect. Unlike most of the girls, her dark hair is cut very short and it clings to her head like a cap. She has a long neck and I can imagine her playing the part of a swan.

"What's your name?" she asks, glancing at me sideways with a small smile.

"Nikolai Maninov."

She glances down at Anton, beside me as always.

"This is my brother, Anton."

"Ivan is bullying him," she says.

I stop so suddenly that several people behind collide with us.

"Can't you tell?" she asks. "He's so quiet. Look at him."

"Why don't you mind your own business?" I snap. "You know nothing about us."

"I know the signs," she says. Her voice is quiet, she has not raised it to match mine and in some place at the back of my mind I admire her for it.

I grasp Anton's hand tighter and walk faster, overtaking a few people to put some distance between us. Bossy, she is. I can see that now. I don't need her to tell me what's wrong with my own brother.

All the same, when my breathing is easier I look down at Anton. "It's not true, is it?"

He doesn't meet my eyes but just gives a slight shake of the head. There! She's wrong. People should mind their own business. I know what's wrong with Anton. He has just lost his father.

By noon we are all exhausted and hungry. Miss Stepovich and one or two of the other teachers are carrying children piggy-back style. I feel sorry for those little ones of five or six. They don't know what is happening to them and probably didn't know why they had ever been sent away from home in the first place.

A lush grassy area by the side of the road is too good to resist and without waiting for permission, we all sink onto the soft bank. I lie back and look at the grey sky.

"I'm hungry." It's Anton. The only words he has spoken the whole morning.

I sit up and open my food package. "Come on, let's eat."

Eat slowly, I say to myself. Enjoy every mouthful. The next food will be harder to come by. But I say none of this to Anton. It's hard enough for *me* to think about. Feeding two hundred children is a huge task. We have no shelter and little money. Winter is approaching. I'm glad I'm not one of the teachers having the responsibility of us all.

What is going to happen to us? My idea begins to take root. Could Anton and I survive on our own? Without him I would certainly go but he is so young and apathy and grief have made him weak.

I curse again under my breath. It isn't fair that I have responsibility for him. Could I leave him? No! That I couldn't do. It had to be both of us or not at all.

Grigori and Boris crawl over to sit with us but we don't talk much.

Talking takes up too much energy and it would mean swallowing our food too quickly. There is a comfort in being with people we know, especially in such a big group.

A few spots of rain splash onto my face and I groan. Miss Stepovich stands up and points towards some trees and everyone scrambles to their feet to run for shelter.

Grigori jumps up too. "Did you hear that?" he shouts. "A train whistle!" He must have better hearing than me because I hadn't heard anything, but a murmur goes through the straggly line of children like a fire through brush.

Grigori and I are on our feet and running. I hear Anton cry out but I ignore him. If we can stop a train perhaps we can get a lift. Two hundred of us? Well, maybe. We have to try.

My feet fly over the ground despite my exhaustion and the sole of my right shoe flapping. Now I can see the puffs of steam rising above the trees and the shiny rails of the track ahead of us.

Grigori begins to fall back but I reach out and catch his sleeve. "Come on!"

We reach the tracks and my legs collapse under me. I look back and see that the whole group is making their way towards us with their bundles on their heads to keep off the rain. The train whistles again and I squint along the track. I can see it now as it turns a bend and bears down on us. I pull off my jacket and wave it as high as I can, having found the strength to get to my feet again.

Under my left foot, which rests on the rail, I can feel the increasing vibration.

"Be careful Nikolai! Get off the track!'" It's Miss Stepovich.

Grigori is on the other side waving too. I can see the engine driver hanging out of his cab. He's seen us and pulls the whistle again, but we are not going to move. We can't walk any further. This train *has* to stop for us.

The squeal of steel against steel as the wheels reverse on the track tells me that it is stopping and when it finally comes to a standstill I can feel the heat from the engine and smell the steam as it looms over us, black and angry.

While Miss Stepovich explains our situation to the driver, everyone climbs aboard. I see him look back along his train and he has no choice but to agree although I never knew what he said. It's a freight train, luckily with many empty wagons and soon they are filled to bursting. Our friends have saved a place for Grigori and me in one of the wagons and we sink onto the hard straw strewn wooden floor as if it is a plush armchair. The animal smell is somehow comforting.

I have no idea where Anton is but know that someone will have looked after him. My body aches all over and I'm hungry again. I have more things on my mind than my little brother. He will have to learn to look after himself a bit more.

We are on our way to Tyumen. For the moment my thoughts of escape are shelved.

Chapter 4

It's dark when we arrive. I stagger to my feet from the cramped position, groaning at my stiff muscles – and they are not new to me by any means. Stiff muscles and exhaustion are things I'm used to, but not like this. Not with hunger cramps and a parched mouth. As I stand up I feel light-headed and have to clutch at the side of the wagon.

I take a deep breath and stumble down onto the track after the others. Some of the little ones are crying and whimpering and the teachers and some of the older girls pick them up. Tatiana is one of them, I notice, and I mentally give her a point although maybe she just wants to impress the teachers.

The townspeople come out of their houses and stare at the long column of children staggering along the road. Some of us got a little sleep on the train but it hasn't helped much.

The teachers approach some of the people and speak to them and many go back into their houses and come out with bread and cheese and water. Some give us apples or pears too and we take it all gratefully. Oh it tastes so good, and the people see our enjoyment and smile understandingly.

I see Tatiana's elegant head above the rest as she comes towards me but it is only when she reaches me that I see she now has Anton with her. She gives me a meaningful look and walks away again. I look down at Anton.

"I had to stop the train," I say, defensively. "You couldn't have run fast enough."

Again the slight movement of the head but without making eye contact with me. I shrug. I'm getting fed up with his silence. I only have so much patience. He presses closer to me and then I see Ivan. He's a few yards in front but has turned round.

"Back with big brother Nikolai," he says in a babyish voice. "Nikolai the train catcher. Our hero! Sprinting across the field despite being tired. Stopping the train single-handed – well, almost." He smirks. "Anyway, you've scored some points with the teachers."

We are holding up the line and Miss Stepovich comes over. "I know you're tired but try and keep moving. There's an old deserted house we're going to stay in for the night."

"It couldn't be worse than that hotel," says Ivan.

"It's not their fault," I say. "They're doing their best for us."

He is wrong. It *is* worse than the hotel. It's shelter, but only just. A great monstrosity of a place, three stories high and built of wood like most of the other houses in Tyumen. Most of the lower and more accessible parts have been stripped away, probably by the people, for firewood. Some of the windows are broken so we stuff the holes with our spare clothes and anything we can find to keep the cold out. Then we each find a small space on the floor, lie down and sleep.

Anton is useful when it comes to begging. He has one of those round cherubic faces with big dark brown eyes that grown-ups always think cute. He has this way of looking up at people, sliding his eyes up, like dogs do when they want something or know they've been naughty and are asking to be forgiven. Anton's a natural, although he doesn't know it.

"We're from the Petrograd children's colony," I say. "We can't get home because of the fighting and we're hungry. Can you spare us some food, please?"

They are short of food as well. How could they not be affected? It is their war too. There doesn't seem to be any young men around so they must have been drafted into the army. I wonder if the actual fighting armies swept through here. No doubt they would have ravaged the place to supply the troops. It must be hard to feed an army on the move.

Nevertheless, even in this desperate place, the poor people at first take pity on us and give us things. Anton only has to give them his soulful look and off they go to fetch something extra. He takes it gratefully but what he can't understand is that we have to share what we get. At the end of the morning we take back to the house all that we've been given and we share it out if it's fruit or bread and cook any vegetables or the occasional piece of meat with lots of water to drink as soup.

Anton is not stupid, he's a normal eight-year old boy, taught to share, but when hunger becomes not just the desire to eat but a griping nagging pain, we all have trouble with the sharing. The only thing which keeps us from eating our spoils is conscience and a certain honour, and there are those who have neither.

One morning we are walking back to the house with two apples and a rabbit. The apples are red and a little dry and shrivelled, definitely past their best but nevertheless very appetising. My mouth waters as I look at them. I tuck the rabbit under one arm and polish the apples on my coat.

Anton reaches up his hand. "Let me carry one, Nikolai."

"Promise me you won't eat it, not even a lick?"

He nods and takes the apple as if it was the most precious thing in the world, holding it cradled in his hand, and staring at it as we walk along. The smell of those apples haunts and tantalises our nostrils but I am proud of him, although I know if I turned my back he would take a bite.

I can feel my apple, round and shiny and I raise my hand to look at it again. It has a small bruise on one side and a bit of stalk still attached. I lick my lips and swallow. Such a small thing an apple. Such a common, taken-for-granted thing. A fruit from a tree, often left to rot on the ground.

My sense of fairness and sharing and setting a good example to Anton disappears in an instant. I am angry. Angry at this war in our country, whatever its justification. There is a bigger war still going on too as far as I know.

I am angry that I gave in to Mother and came on this trip. I'm not angry at her any more, only at myself and the world.

It isn't fair!

Our group is only a fraction of the number of children in the Petrograd Children's colony. I heard that there are eight hundred of us altogether. If the others are still alive, they will be doing the same as us, begging, begging, from people who have nothing themselves.

I grab Anton's collar and pull him into a side street. Then I take his hand and push the apple towards his mouth.

"Eat!" I say.

He looks up at me confused, as if he can't believe what he is hearing.

"For once let's break the rules. Sometimes it's every man for himself." And I bite into my apple. A big bite, not a small cut up piece. I open my mouth as wide as I can and bite off a chunk with a satisfying smack.

"Caught you!" says a voice.

Chapter 5

It is Ivan.

Out of all the people who could have caught us it is Ivan and his friend Karl. They stand there grinning at us. I hate the way Ivan's mouth turns up in one corner.

They snatch the apples out of our hands and devour them in a couple of bites, saliva and juice running down the corners of their mouths, licking their lips in an exaggerated way, all the time watching our faces and grinning.

Then Ivan puts his face really close to mine and I can smell the apple on his breath. I am so hungry that if he offered me the pickings from his teeth I would eat them.

"You are supposed to be sharing what you get," he says. "Not eating it yourselves. And here we were thinking you were a nice boy looking after your baby brother and all the time you're a cheat."

"Cheat yourself, Ivan," I say.

He sniggers. "Oh but we *are* sharing, aren't we Karl? I give things to him and he gives things to me." They both laugh. Then Ivan's face goes serious. Really serious.

"And in future you'll share with us. All right? Half of what you get you give to us?"

"Why should I?"

"Because if you don't, we'll just keep teasing your little brother here, and we can tell – he doesn't like it much, do you Shrimp?"

I've never seen Anton looking so terrified. So Tatiana had been right. He *was* being bullied.

"All right," I say. "Half."

Half of what? Sometimes we don't get anything at all now and who could blame the people? What little they have left they are keeping for themselves. Even Ivan seems to realise that, though one day when we are given a chicken he lets us take it back to the house on one condition – that I steal another one for them.

I do it that night.

The house where the chicken came from is very small and modest. It is not a farm but the old man and his wife keep chickens in a small coop at the back of the house. I haven't seen them but heard them clucking when we went to the front door.

"Don't come again," the man had said, though not in a harsh way. "I'm sorry, but we can't spare any more. Good luck to you all."

I hated stealing from him but I was going to have to get used to it. That's what it had come to, even without Ivan.

Stealing. Something we are taught is wrong from infancy. Now we steal or we die. That is the simple choice.

Snow is beginning to fall as I creep round the side of the house and I can't control my shaking, both with fear and with cold. Summer clothes – even several layers of them – are nothing against Siberian winters, and this is only the end of November.

I've had no experience with chickens at all. The only sort I know are dead ones from the butcher, and even then they're a rare luxury at Christmas or other special times. As I open the latch of their run I can see faint movements inside the henhouse as they shuffle restlessly and cluck with anxiety.

As far as I can tell there are three of them, perching on a wooden bar. As I draw closer one of them squawks and flutters off the perch onto the ground. That's the one I'll go after. I'm thinking that I'll take off my jacket and throw it over the chicken. After that I'll have to kill it, somehow.

I'm very light on my feet. That's what I'm good at. But I'm no match for this chicken. As I run one way it dodges between my feet. Every time I throw my jacket and think I have it, it squawks loudly and scrambles away, leaving me with a handful of feathers.

The noise a chicken can make is unbelievable and eventually a flickering light appears in an upstairs window of the house.

Was it better to face the man as a thief and be shamed or face Ivan and friends? There is no choice really. Thieving was to become our means of survival so we had to get used to the shame. I had to protect Anton.

I dive for the chicken. This is my last chance. I fall on it with all my weight and it screeches horribly and stops struggling. I feel its bones break under me and it makes me feel sick.

"Who is it?" the man shouts. He hasn't stopped to light a lamp but has come outside with a candle which flickers and goes out. I hear him curse as I run, the chicken bundled up in my jacket. I hope there is no blood or anything else all over it.

On the way home I have an idea.

Miss Stepovich looks me up and down. "It's not for you, Nikolai. Maybe more for the older boys."

I shake my head. "No, I can do it. I'm strong."

"But you're such a slender boy, Nikolai, even without being half starved. I hear that you're a student at the Academy."

"Yes, that's right." But heaven help me if Ivan finds out. "But I'm strong. You have to be."

She smiles in a tired way and nods. I notice how her clothes hang on her now. The waist of her skirt is tied with string to stop it from falling down and I know that she is eating as little as we are, if not less.

Anton and I set out at six the next morning. We, or at least I, am going to try and get a job on a farm.

It is still dark but I can see stars so it's a clear sky. Very still, no wind, but the cold cuts through our thin clothes like an icy sword.

The town is quiet as we walk through. I put my arm around Anton's shoulder and hold him close to try and retain our body heat. As usual he says nothing. Is this what it would be like if we took off on our own?

I choose a place quite a distance from the town and unlikely to have had too many beggars. All the more distance for us to walk each day though.

The snow in front of the main door is flat and untrodden so we go round to the back and knock on an old wooden door which is dry and crumbling at the edges through exposure to the weather.

"Who is it?" comes a woman's voice from inside.

"We're starving," I shout. "But we're not here to beg. We want to work for our food."

The handle turns and the door opens a crack. I can see part of a face in the dim light of the lamp she is holding up. Somewhere behind her a dog whines.

"I have hardly enough for myself," the woman says, then corrects herself. "We... have very little either."

I can see her eyes as she tries to get a better look at us without leaving herself too vulnerable. Then she sees Anton and that does the trick again. The door opens wider.

She is about the same age as my mother and there are other similarities too. Her brown hair is traditionally long and plaited into two braids which frame her head like a crown and her blue eyes have a gentle quality. There the similarities to mother cease. Her hands, as she reaches out to touch Anton's head, are calloused and the nails ragged. I know the signs now. I might be from the city but I have come to know and respect these hard-working peasants.

She must like my face too, even though fortunately it isn't cute like Anton's, because she beckons us inside. The dog creeps under the table and watches us warily, lacking the energy to bark.

"I heard about your children's colony from Petrograd," she says. "Everyone's talking about you and cursing the day you came to Tyumen. First the soldiers pillaged the town and now we are made to feel guilty at the sight of starving children."

"We cannot get home," I say. "It would mean crossing through the battle lines."

She nods, and indicates that we should sit on the bed in the corner. There are no chairs, no doubt long gone into the fire, and although there is a table, that will probably be next. It is warm in the kitchen by the woodstove. The first time we have been warm in a long time. The smell of baking bread almost masks the underlying musty dampness and there is a distinct odour of animals too. Besides the bed and the table there is a stone sink and a large, half-empty basket of logs next to the stove. Some ragged grey items of underwear hang on a string suspended above the stove and when she sees me looking, she snatches them down in embarrassment.

"You are really all the way from Petrograd?" Her voice holds a hint of awe.

I nod and she stares away into the distance as if trying to imagine how different it is there to here.

"They are starving too," I say, destroying her mental image.

"I am alone here," she admits. "I could use some help with the animals and chopping firewood. I will feed you, but I can't give you any money. My husband is away fighting."

I glance at Anton. "Our father was killed in the great war last April," I say. Was it really nine months ago?

The woman goes to the stove and ladles out a clear liquid into two bowls.

"Here, this will warm you. You can borrow some winter clothes of my husband's too." She points to Anton. "He should stay behind in future. He is too young to work and he will get under my feet here."

I clear the snow from her path and chop some firewood that day. She has some logs stacked up but very few, and when they are gone it will be impossible to get any more. The snow is too thick to go into the forest and I have no means of chopping down trees. All the smaller ones will have already gone.

Everyone is in the same plight. The whole town is starving to death.

After that Anton stays at the house and I can only hope that Ivan leaves him alone, as long as I supply him with food. The woman gives me a small meal at noon and then something to eat on the way back at the end of the day. This I take back and give half to Ivan before sharing the rest with everyone else, but a crust of bread and a chunk of cheese don't go far amongst two hundred people.

Several others have got work too, in return for food, but it is obvious to we older ones and no doubt the adults, that we cannot support the whole colony. It is like a slow death. Some have become experts at scavenging and stealing and disappear every morning despite the temperatures being well below freezing. In the evenings we return and share our spoils, whether ill-gotten or honestly gained.

Many children, especially the younger ones, have neither the energy nor any reason to venture out and crouch apathetically around the stoves and fireplaces.

But it isn't long before Ivan gets to know about the goats.

Chapter 6

Even he, with his cockiness and menace, is human in so far as he suffers like the rest of us. From the big, rather beefy youth he has become thin and stooped. His face is gaunt and, like all of us, his hair has thinned. I have only ever seen him in the same clothes and these are now torn rags, hardly covering his body. He has somehow acquired a piece of old coarse brown blanket and cut a hole in it for his head. That is what keeps out a little of the cold. Also, like the rest of us, he is filthy.

But the old Ivan is still in there.

"I hear she has a goat," he says one evening towards the end, to my reckoning, of December.

My heart sinks. I know who he means by 'she'. Mrs Alexandrova, the lady I work for.

"It's a poor thin thing," I say. "It's a nanny goat and gives milk – or did."

"Steal it," he says, just like that.

I open my mouth to protest but he grabs my shirt with surprising strength.

It is all she has, that goat. The thin trickle of milk it gives helps sustain her life and I do not want to take it away, especially after all she has done for me.

But I know that I have no choice. Anton is very weak. He can't take the bullying on top of the starvation and the teachers have lost the will and strength to discipline anybody. Gradually the strongest are taking over. Soon there will be anarchy.

This will have to be my last day at work. There isn't much I can do anyway, I am too weak myself. Even walking there and back utterly exhausts me so that I creep onto my floor space at night sometimes not expecting to wake up in the morning.

My limbs are just sticks and I stare at them in dismay. I no longer recognise them as part if me. It's as if the legs of some other skinny kid have been stuck onto my body. I'm not slender and light on my feet any more either, nor am I a promising student in the Academy. I'm a walking skeleton waiting to die. One day people will come and find two hundred bodies strewn around an old wooden house and wonder who we were.

This house has become a skeleton too as we have plundered its wooden walls for firewood. It's a vicious circle. The more wood we take from the walls to burn the more exposed we are to the weather.

On my last day at the farm I chop the remaining firewood. It takes me four hours to do what I could once have done in half an hour. I have to keep having rests and each time it becomes more difficult to get up and start again.

Mrs Alexandrova seems to sense a finality. Perhaps she has given up trying too. Her store of corn from the last harvest is all used up. The seven goats which she had when I started work here are reduced to one.

And she has eaten her dog.

We say goodbye in the late afternoon. She hugs me to her and wishes me luck. She smells like my mother and it's a long time since anyone has hugged me.

"Thank you, Nikolai." Her voice is weak and there's a tremor in it. "Good luck."

I feel sick at what I am about to do. To betray this woman seems the worst thing in the world. I can't do it. Tears well up in my eyes. It's a long time since I have cried, I didn't, even when my father died. Maybe that's all part of it. Everything piling up until it's too much to hold in. I cry as she holds me close and makes soothing noises like a mother to a child.

Later I leave without looking back. It's dark now and I know she's standing at the door watching because the yellow light from her lamp is shining the way for me. As soon as it goes out I turn back.

I wish the goat was difficult to steal. I wish it would put up a struggle like the chicken, but when I untie it, it just follows me silently out of the yard without a sound. The struggle is within me. I have never done anything so terrible in all my life, and all because of Ivan. One day I will get even with him. One day. If we survive.

All that night, instead of sleeping I lie awake, exhausted as I am. I picture Mrs Alexandrova going out to milk the goat and finding it gone. Of course anyone could have taken it but I know that she will know it was me. It would be asking too much to expect her to forgive me.

Ivan took the goat and has hidden it somewhere. Somehow no-one saw us. No doubt he and his friends will have a good feast. I hope they are all sick. Then it would be a waste, unless they get down on their hands and knees and eat their own vomit.

At least that is the end of it. No more giving half of what I get. No more paying to stop him bullying Anton.

No more anything.

But the next morning he drags me from sleep.

"Nikolai! Wake up. There's something you have to do."

I get up and follow them, he and Karl. My heart is racing as I know it is something bad. I can tell by his renewed energy, by the evil spark in his eyes. By the spring in his step.

They lead me outside to the back of the house where there's an old outhouse. Most of it has gone, the bit that was made of wood. All that's left is part of a stone wall with a rough piece of slate roof full of holes.

The goat is standing inside, shivering, since the icy wind cuts right through the open structure. Or is it fear?

Ivan shoves me forward towards the goat.

"Kill it," he says.

Chapter 7

"Well we can't eat it like that!" he says in mock surprise as I gape at him. "Alive and furry. Finish the job. Kill it."

"How?"

"Well, any way you like. The choice is yours. And don't take all day. We're hungry."

"I've never killed anything..." I begin.

"Oh yes you have. You killed the chicken. This is no different."

It *is* different. I'd accidentally killed the chicken by falling on it, which had saved me from having to do it in cold blood, like this.

Ivan and Karl sink into a corner. I can see that they are very weak too and can't stand for long. Maybe I should just walk away. What could they do? For myself it is no problem. We are all going to die anyway. Starvation itself is agony. No-one who has never been really hungry has any idea what it is like. The pain in your insides invades your every thought. It feels as though you are gnawing away at your own flesh, which is really what is happening. You are consuming your own flesh. You can hardly think of anything else.

Ivan's taunts can wash over me now, I don't care, even if he finds out my biggest secret. The dream of my great future will remain a dream now anyway.

But I can't let Anton suffer any more than he already has and I know that Ivan's need for food will drive him to extreme lengths. It is far easier to tease a small boy than kill a goat.

I look round the outhouse for a suitable weapon rather than just strangle it to death. That would be too slow and I might not even be strong enough.

There's an old sickle on the wall but it's rusty and blunt. Next to it is a pair of shears for shearing sheep. I walk over and look at them. They are rusty too but they have pointed ends.

I unhook them from the nail on the wall and a shower of red rust sprinkles orange over my hand. I test the points with my finger. This will do. Now I have the means but need the strength.

Ivan and Karl are watching me through tired eyes. Ivan licks his lips in a lazy manner and smiles slightly.

The goat is still shivering in the corner and I walk towards it, grasping the shears tighter and pulling the two blades together into one double blade. Quick, that's the only way, both for it and for me. Before I can think about it any more I grasp its horns with my left hand and plunge the shears into its neck.

I shall never forget the sound that goat makes as it dies. It is almost human. I feel the shears go through the tough skin and hit bone at the back, its spine I suppose.

This time I am sick although there is little in my stomach. I retch and heave in horrible uncontrollable spasms, still holding the bloody shears.

The goat does not die quickly. It takes a few gurgling breaths and slowly sinks to the ground where it lies twitching for a while. I just hope it is not conscious.

When I have finished retching I skin it, knowing that is what Ivan would have asked next. I have to do this terrible thing all in one go without stopping. When it's done, I leave them to their feast. They tear away handfuls of the goat's flesh and eat it raw, the blood dripping down their chins.

My mouth waters at the sight.

New Year comes and goes without celebration and Russian Christmas is approaching although since the Revolution last year it has been banned. But who is there to report us?

A couple of evenings before our Christmas, a few of the girls try to rouse us into singing some carols. Tatiana leads them and I mentally give her another point.

We sing *Joy to the World* and *Jingle Bells* in a pathetic whisper and quickly lose interest.

But whether or not Christmas is banned, on January 6th 1919, Russian Christmas Eve, Santa Claus arrives.

His name is Riley Allen and he's American. He pushes open the door and finds us all huddled in two rooms.

We stare in astonishment at this man standing upright in his smart uniform, clean and well fed. We have almost forgotten what normal people look like. He has a round boyish face and a broad smile.

"I'm from the American Red Cross," he says. "I've been looking for you."

Miss Stepovich staggers to her feet. "You've been looking for us?"

He nods. "The American people are going to look after you. We'll bring food and warm clothing and wood for the fire."

Miss Stepovich translates this to us and we can't believe it. Grigori looks at me questioningly as if wanting to confirm that this man is real and not an hallucination brought on by near death. I nod and smile. Anton lifts his head.

"This man has come to save us," I say, and he frowns as if unable to comprehend such a thing. Then he whispers. "Is it Santa Claus?"

I laugh and others turn to look at me as if I'm mad. No-one has laughed here for a long time and it's a strange sound.

"It *is* Santa Claus!" I say. "Merry Christmas!" And we all join in the laughter and wish each other a very Happy Christmas whether it is banned or not. For us it is the best Christmas we have ever had.

Now I really understand what they mean by 'the basic needs of human beings'. Without any one of them – shelter, warmth, food and water – you die. It's as simple as that. But given those four things humans can make a miraculous recovery from near death.

That's how it was with Anton and many others. Mr Allen and his colleagues brought us clothes, food and firewood and patched up the house a little and now it is alive again and shuddering under the onslaught of many small feet and young voices.

We laugh again. Despite everything, we can laugh.

I think we all feel invincible. I can cope with anything now, even Ivan. I am sure we shall be going home soon. America is a big powerful country. It can get us through the battle lines.

But it turns out I am wrong. In the spring Mr Allen calls us together and says that the military positions are changing. We are in danger of being in the middle of the front line again. We will have to move on. But where?

East to Vladivostok. Over four thousand miles from Petrograd and our families. We have had one letter from mother in all the time we've been away. She didn't mention the letters we had sent so she couldn't have received them. She hasn't had my apology. She said she's all right, that there is a little food if you stand in line long enough. She is lying just like I lied to her in my letters. I wonder if I will ever see her again.

Chapter 8

It isn't until July that the three trains arrive to take us to Vladivostok. It's the day after my birthday.

Before we leave Tyumen there is something I want to do. I visit the kitchen in the old house and beg for any food scraps which are not worth taking with us. I leave them in an old cooking pot on Mrs Alexandrova's doorstep and hope it will in some way pay her back for the goat. I don't even know if she is still alive.

We meet up with the rest of the Petrograd Children's Colony so that we are now eight hundred altogether and begin our long trek across Siberia.

Sometimes we run out of coal for the trains and have to beg or trade for more. Sometimes we run out of track where it has been torn up by the Red partisans and we have to wait for it to be repaired.

But we finally get there.

When I first see where we are going to live in Vladivostok I think it looks like a prison.

"I hope it has some sort of heating," I say to Grigori and Boris as we stare out across Golden Horn Bay at the stone buildings. I expect them to laugh as we stand there on this warm September day but no-one will forget last winter for a long time.

Anton seems quite excited. He has begun to talk again – more like his old self.

"It's on an island," he says and I groan at the stating of the obvious, and look down at him. Sometimes he can be so irritating.

"Why don't you stick with boys your own age, " I say. "Do you have to follow me round like a dog?"

"He's all right."

It's all very well for Boris, he hasn't any brothers or sisters.

"Come on you boys." Mr Bramhall, one of Mr Allen's assistants, is waving to us from the boat and we climb aboard for our trip over to Russian Island.

Our accommodation is an old barracks which once housed the Tsar's navy, Riley Allen tells us. No-one knows who owns it now, and it's vacant, so that is where we are going.

For how long? Who knows. Until our stupid soldiers stop fighting each other. I wonder what life will be like afterwards and how different it will be depending on who wins. I don't understand much about politics.

Some work has been done on the barracks to make them suitable for us and some Red Cross volunteers are arriving from America to help out. I like Americans and have decided that I will try and learn some English so I can talk directly to them, especially to Riley Allen. I really want to talk to him and tell him about my father. They would have been about the same age. I want to ask him why he came all the way from Hawaii to help us here. He showed us pictures of Hawaii and I can hardly believe there is anywhere like that, so very different from anywhere I have ever seen. Beautiful sandy beaches and palm trees and he says that the weather is hot but not too hot and that the water is clear so you can go out in a boat and watch all the tropical fish. My father would have loved that because he kept tropical fish in a tank in our apartment and he knew all about where they came from. He and Riley Allen would have really got on, I'm sure.

Although there are eight hundred of us we tend to stick together with people we know, just occasionally making new friends. I haven't seen much of Tatiana lately and hear that she is helping the new volunteers. Trust her. Always has to be in the middle of things.

We are in barracks with others our age which means that Anton and I are split up and I worry about him a bit and watch his face for what Tatiana would call 'the signs.'

"Brothers are all right," I say to Boris and Grigori, " but like all good things you can have too much of them. But," I add, "they *are* better than sisters."

They can't comment. They have neither, but they both have a mother *and* a father. Grigori's father is a farrier and Boris drives us silly telling us about his father's automobile and motor cycle servicing business and that soon there will be no more horse drawn vehicles on the streets. I haven't had much experience with horses and don't want to, either. Chickens and goats are enough.

We settle into a routine again. Lessons, recreation, good food and the occasional trip into the city. The older ones are allowed more freedom than us and I hear that Ivan and Karl have been in trouble with Riley Allen over something and that Ivan threatened him. At least he was picking on someone his own size.

Towards the end of November Miss Stepovich calls together all those children over fifteen.

"We want you to look for work," she says. "You are old enough to begin a trade of some sort. I have already spoken to the authorities at the hospital and they will train some of you girls who want to be nurses. Several other companies are willing to take on trainees too. Tell us what your interests are and we shall try to fit you to a suitable job."

There's a mixed reception to this idea. Some want to go to university and follow professions and are not willing to do what they see as menial jobs.

Me? I know what I am going to do and there is no opportunity for it here in Vladivostok.

"Nikolai?" Miss Stepovich's steady gaze waits for an answer. I shake my head.

"But you can't continue your studies as a …"

"No!" I didn't mean to shout but couldn't let her divulge my secret to all these… strangers, or to Ivan. I sense him, although I can't actually see him, over to my left.

"As a what?" he says.

His interest in me has been reawakened. He never misses anything. Now there is a reason for him to dig away until he finds out.

"A clown," I say. "I want to join the circus."

Everyone laughs but I know he isn't fooled. I turn my head cockily and look him straight in the eye and he has a quizzical look on his face.

Miss Stepovich ignores my outburst and I think what a really nice understanding person she is. She obviously realises why I want to keep my ambition from the likes of Ivan. He could make my life hell.

The matter is dropped for the moment, as far as I am concerned. I must think about it, she says.

In the meantime preparations are made to celebrate, if not Christmas, then the New Year. We decorate a tree and the younger ones make coloured paper chains to hang on it. At the top we place two flags, an American one and a Russian one but the American one doesn't last long. Someone removes it and sets fire to it, leaving a little pile of ashes in the middle of the floor. I never hear that there is any sort of investigation into who did it but I know that there are a number of older members of the colony who think Riley and his associates are not to be trusted and have ulterior motives.

Tatiana speaks to me one day.

"I hear you are good at dancing," she says. "Will you take part in our concert please?"

I stare at her. Who had let it out? Miss Stepovich? Surely not. No! It must have been Anton, that little tell-tale!

"Well?" she says. "Is it true or not? I haven't seen you at any of our Saturday dances."

To hell with it. Tell the world. I don't care any more. This is my ambition and I should be proud of it.

"It's not that kind of dancing," I say. "I do ballet."

I have to say – and it's another point to her – that I might as well have told her that I played football. Not a muscle of her face twitches, not in a negative way, anyway. She just nods, smiles and says:

"That's perfect. Can we count on you, then?"

Before I know it I'm saying yes and panicking about not being fit and mentally assigning time morning and evening to get in trim. It's nearly two years since I had had my last lesson.

I feel elated, yet I am still angry with Anton for his betrayal. In one way I have been released like a bird to fly again, and in another I have to put on my heavy suit of armour against Ivan and those who will be quick to mock a boy dancer. I know the names they call us.

Another thing happened this month. Since the railway to the west was disrupted there is no way of getting any mail through to Petrograd so it's been months since any of us have heard any news from home. Then Riley Allen had an idea. He has arranged for it to go by ship east to America and then across the Atlantic to Europe to Estonia. Then it goes overland to Russia.

He really is a great man. He can move mountains.

Anton and I write to mother. He reads and writes very well now and is learning some English like me.

The concert is on December 7th.

Chapter 9

I decide to perform a dance from *The Nutcracker*. I play one of the toys but having no costume just dance in my ordinary clothes and bare feet. It is wonderful dancing again, though my performance is probably not very good because I haven't danced for so long. I worry about how much I have lost my suppleness and balance.

The joy in dancing is almost worth the heckling. Even though the teachers and Riley Allen and everyone try to stop it, I can hear them.

"Look at him! Poncing around on his toes like a sissy! Is that all you can do, Nikolai? Dance like a girl?"

Ivan is shouting the loudest. He's really enjoying himself.

Apart from him there is a mixed reception. People can't always accept boys or men dancing ballet. I should be used to it by now but it always hurts. Can't they see how hard it is? How strong we have to be to lift the ballerina with such ease? Can't they see the skill and beauty?

When it's over I go back to my seat and watch the rest of the show. There's a lot of talent amongst all these children.

"Thank you, Nikolai." Tatiana smiles and I smile back.

"I didn't notice *you* up there."

"I'm no good at anything. I play the piano a bit but…" she shrugs and spreads her arms. "No piano."

"You'd make a good dancer," I say. "You're tall and slender you have an elegance in the way you move."

Surprisingly she blushes and I can't believe I've just said what I said.

"No." She shakes her head. "I'm too old now, aren't I? Fourteen? I have other ambitions."

She doesn't tell me what they are and I don't ask. She sees someone she has to talk to and turns away.

Later some musicians from the city play Russian music for us to dance. Everyone is very happy this evening. We forget about the war for a while as we whirl and skip or clap to the lively rhythms as well as watching others. Riley Allen and Burl Bramhall try to do a Cossack dance and we laugh a lot when they keep falling over.

"My father is good at that," says Boris beside me. "You should see him."

We are silent for a moment as I think of my father and I guess he is thinking of his. Mine certainly hadn't been good at dancing but he had had other talents. He used to make us laugh a lot. He was a good mimic and could do lots of voices, including friends and relatives of ours.

"My father can do those Cossack kicks for half a minute," Boris says. "He was once the champion of the whole province. Thirty seconds!" he emphasises.

I know. I have heard it all before.

"Should be useful when he's starting those motor cycles," I say, and could have bitten my tongue off. Starting Boris off about motor cycles and engines is a dangerous thing. We could be here all night.

"Did I tell you my father has a 1915 twin cylinder Pope?"

I nod but he carries on just the same. "It's got front and rear suspension and can do sixty miles an hour!"

I'm amazed at the thought of that speed but I dare not show too much enthusiasm. I tug at his sleeve.

"Come on, Boris. Let's get some food."

Ivan never misses an opportunity to goad me about my dancing. He's like a dog with a bone. I try to ignore him but each time it happens I resolve that one day I will get even. I still watch Anton for any signs of bullying but hope that while I am fair game he will leave Anton alone. He probably isn't bright enough to be able to do two things at once.

Luckily he's been sent to work ashore, as have many of the older ones, so I don't bump into him too often. Boris has work too, not as an automobile mechanic as he wanted, but on the docks helping load and unload ships. Grigori and I have been given work in the barracks so we hardly get to go ashore. He is helping in the kitchen and I work in the food storage area.

Anton is becoming more independent and I appreciate him more in small doses.

It's very cold but now we have warm clothes and plenty of food so we can't complain. We're used to cold winters. We've been away from home nearly two years now and wonder when we'll be able to go back.

Riley Allen keeps us informed about everything he's doing. In the middle of February he says he hopes we shall be able to go home within two months. Two months! That will go in no time. He says he's trying to arrange for four trains and already has one waiting but he needs the go ahead from the American Red Cross authorities.

I am sure that will come soon. Then we can go home!

Chapter 10

Riley Allen told us that he hopes that the Bolsheviks will soon be in control of the Trans Siberian Railway and will allow us to go back to Petrograd, but those working in the city report more and more Japanese troops pouring in as allied troops evacuate Siberia.

One morning as I climb out of bed and look out of the window across to the city, I can see Japanese flags fluttering from many buildings. Then just as the door to the dormitory is flung open and Burl Bramhall yells "Get down!" we hear gunfire. It looks as though the war is determined to follow us wherever we go.

No-one goes to the mainland to work today except the girls who are working as nurses at the hospital. They come back reporting a city full of victorious Japanese soldiers waving their rifles in triumph.

Riley Allen goes round with a worried look on his boyish face and he and the other Red Cross workers and our teachers are having many meetings.

Not for the first time they don't know what to do with us.

"They'll abandon us," says Ivan loudly, as we eat dinner in the dining room. "Save their own skins."

"Shut up!" says Grigori. "That's probably what you would do in his situation but he won't do that."

"You watch," says Karl, "As soon as the Bolsheviks get here they'll be gone and so will I."

"Don't forget to ask the Japanese authorities first," I say. "It looks like they're in control here."

"And what would you know, nancy boy?"

My fingers tighten round my fork and I stab at the sausage on my plate. One day, Ivan. One day…

The plan, when it comes, is so staggering that none of us can speak. It's an idea so unbelievable and beyond our comprehension that there is silence in the dining hall for a full minute. Then pandemonium breaks out.

Riley Allen and his staff have come up with the only possible plan to get us home. Instead of going west, we are going east, right round the world, like our mail. The long way home.

Riley stands with his head bowed waiting for the noise to cease. At last most people stop talking and look across at him, except Ivan, Karl and several others who thump their fists on the table.

"Do you have a better idea, gentlemen?" asks Burl Bramhall.

"Yes, we wait until we're rescued by our people," yells Karl. "We've known all along that you had other motives. You want to take us to America and use us as forced labour. We're not stupid."

Ivan's beefy face is suffused with anger. "You can't make us go," he shouts. "You can't force us onto your ship."

I have to admire Burl Bramhall. He doesn't get angry or shout back. He just nods slightly. "Your objection is noted, gentlemen. We can discuss it later when things are more definite. We don't even have a ship yet."

Well, as far as I'm concerned they can leave those four behind and good riddance. They say there are always one or two bad apples in a barrel and I don't know why I should have the bad luck to be near them.

She is called the *Yomei Maru*.

Many of us come out to watch her arrival on July 9th as she sails into Golden Bay. She's a Japanese freighter on her maiden voyage but doesn't look like anything much to me and I've seen a lot of ships in Petrograd. For one thing she doesn't look big enough for all of us. She's sort of long and low with one thin straight stack in the centre on which is painted a red cross. Nothing much to look at. On the side are three enormous words painted in red. I think one of them says 'American' so I guess the others are 'Red Cross'.

"Where are we all going to sleep?" asks Anton. "There aren't any cabins."

Good question.

"They've refitted her," I say. "Made lots of changes to accommodate us. Our beds will probably be in the holds where they usually store the cargo."

"I don't want to go." I look down at Anton and there is fear in his eyes.

"You want to stay behind with Ivan?" I ask.

"It will be an adventure," Boris says. He hates it when I tease Anton. "When we get home we'll have been all the way round the world."

I snort. "Crammed in like a can of sardines," I say. "They have lots of fun."

Grigori nudges me to shut me up. "At least we'll be moving towards home."

"Away from home," says Anton. "How can away from home be towards home?"

"It can," I say, trying to keep my patience, "because the earth is round. If you keep going in one direction you will eventually arrive back where you started."

"The only thing is," puts in Boris, "how long is eventually?"

None of us knows the answer to that.

Someone is tugging at my arm and I shake it off irritably. It's the middle of the night. I'm tired. People are shouting. I open my eyes and raise my head off the pillow.

"What's happening?"

"The ship's on fire." Anton is kneeling on his bed looking out of the window. It seems I'm the last to know because everyone is crowding round behind him, trying to get a good view.

I throw back the covers and go and join them, still blinking the sleep out of my eyes and yawning.

She's alight all right. Her after deck is well ablaze and black smoke swirls into the air. It's quite spectacular. A fire boat arrives and soon a jet of water is being aimed at the heart of the blaze.

As we watch there's a sudden flare and then a large piece of canvas partly breaks free and flaps and blazes for a few moments before detaching itself completely and drifting down to the water where it goes out.

After the fire is out we all crawl back to bed but I don't think anybody sleeps much. It's only five o'clock but dawn is breaking and I, for one, am worried about how much damage had been done. Will the ship still be sea worthy? How long will the repairs take? Despite others' doubts I have complete faith in Riley Allen and the American Red Cross. I trust their word.

It turned out to be Ivan, Karl and a couple of their friends. Surprise, surprise! He might be a loud mouth but is a bit short on brains. They had somehow got aboard the ship without being seen, and set alight to the surplus coal stacked on deck. Then they had returned leaving a nice set of coal dust footprints leading back to their dormitory and even though there are twenty of them sleeping there it didn't take long to weed them out.

Riley Allen says the ship was not badly damaged and no-one was hurt. I must admit that while we were watching the fire I'd forgotten that the crew were on board. The fire hadn't had time to spread further than the coal. Some canvas sails had been rigged up near the hold hatchways to catch the wind and direct it downwards for ventilation, and it was one of those we had seen ablaze. Easy to replace but more expense.

Burl Bramhall calls us together that afternoon and tells us all about it. I like him, he's good at settling disputes and is always having a joke with us, but he isn't joking this time. He says we are all their responsibility and that he and Riley Allen are committed to getting us back home – and that means *all* of us. We are all minors and do not have the choice of going or not. That reminded me about my thoughts of escape but there is no point now.

Some of us think they should lock those boys up until we sail but they don't, and the next morning we hear that they tried to steal a life-boat. One of the crew heard the davits creaking and caught them.

Either they learnt their lesson or ran out of ideas but Ivan didn't try anything else and it's now the day before departure. We are excited in a way but a bit apprehensive too. None of the people I have spoken to have ever been on a ship before. I'd love to tell my father about it all.

We are all packed – not that we have much to pack! Anton wasn't around so I did his too. I asked if we could have bunks together. Miss Stepovich said they *were* trying to keep siblings together – whatever that means.

By lights out, Anton still hasn't turned up and I go to look for him. I try to remember if he told me he was doing anything special but even then he should be back by now. Sometimes he can be such a pest. Sometimes I wish I was an only child like Grigori and Boris. Life would be so much simpler.

I can't find him. No-one had seen him since lunchtime. I go to find Miss Stepovich.

At the same time Riley Allen receives a note from Ivan.

Chapter 11

I take back what I thought about Anton being a pest and about wishing I was an only child. He can be a pest anytime. I wish he *would* be a pest. Right now. But he can't because Ivan and friends have him hostage. They will only let him go if Riley Allen gives them a boat and provisions.

I beg them to do that. Where would they go in a boat, anyway? The Japanese have restricted traffic in and out of the city. Who cares what happens to those four? We might have some peace on our voyage without them. The answer is simple, I say, give them a boat and get Anton back.

But Riley Allen shakes his head in such a definite sort of way that I know there is no persuading him and I get angry. Maybe Ivan is right in thinking they have other reasons for seeming to help us, otherwise why would they insist on taking everyone? So there would be no witnesses? No-one left behind to tell what happened?

I shake his hand off my shoulder and walk out.

"Anton will be all right," says Boris, back in the dormitory.

I turn on him. "You're always criticising me for being impatient with him and teasing him and now you think he'll be all right with Ivan?" I can feel heat rising in my face. "Riley Allen is not going to give them a boat. That means they will not release Anton."

"They'll have to in the end," says Grigori. "They won't want him with them."

Grigori was right but I didn't want to think about the alternative. Surely even Ivan wouldn't go that far?

"We don't even know where they are," I say, choking on the words.

Boris sits down on his bed facing me. "They must be somewhere on the island," he says. "They can't have gone ashore, someone would have remembered. They'd have been seen on the boat."

I just shake my head. Why doesn't Riley Allen mount a search of the island? Flush them out. Get Anton. Anton is all that matters. I don't care about those boys. They've been nothing but trouble all along and I can't understand why anyone would care about them at all.

I can't sleep. I wonder how they are treating Anton. He's been really happy lately, more self assured. Mother will be surprised – if we ever see her again. Sometimes it's hard to remember what she looks like. That scares me. I remember my father though. The last time we saw him. He kissed us all and walked quickly out of the apartment. He'd had a few days leave but wouldn't talk about the war even though we'd asked. He'd been very quiet, not at all like his usual self.

Anton and I had run to the window and waved to him as he walked down the street and I remember he stopped and looked back once, his face pale, his uniform worse for wear. He'd slowly raised his hand in a half salute and then stood looking at us for a minute before turning and briskly marching away. His face was burned into my memory.

But mother? She hadn't come to the window to wave. She had sat down quietly in her chair, I remember that now, though I hadn't thought about it at the time. She'd sat perfectly still staring at nothing, her fingers gripping the arms of the chair until her knuckles turned white. We had turned from the window and Anton had asked her something – I can't remember what – but she hadn't answered, hadn't even heard. I can remember it all now but still can't quite see her face.

If only father was here. He would know what to do.

At five I am up and standing at the window. The *Yomei Maru* looks as though she has steam up ready to go. I can see the crew busy on the deck erecting another canvas sail in front of the starboard hatch. A coal barge is replenishing the coal heap from the seaward side.

At breakfast we are all given a metal tag with a number on to hang around our necks. I am number twenty two. It was Burl Bramhall's idea to keep track of us during the voyage when we went ashore. We are to board and disembark the ship in numerical order.

I look at my tag as I swing it on my finger. There is no way I am getting on that ship before Anton is back.

Burl comes up to me and whispers: "Don't worry, we have a plan." He gives me another tag – number twenty-three, for Anton.

But I am sceptical.

After lunch they start to board everyone. My number soon comes up but I stand resolutely by the gangplank and refuse to board. Even Riley cannot persuade me and I even threaten to throw my numbered disc into the water. Finally the rules are broken and they go from number twenty-one to number twenty-four.

It's a hot day and standing in the sun all that time I begin to feel dizzy and sit down on an iron bollard. Riley Allen himself brings me a drink of water. He doesn't say anything but he looks pleased with himself.

When everyone is on board the decks are swarming with children looking for their bunks or just exploring. I can see Boris and Grigori leaning over the rail of the bows. They wave and point to something on the other side of the ship that I can't yet see.

A small boat comes nosing round and draws up further down where there is a small jetty. She has one sail and is being rowed by two men. Riley Allen appears near her and the men step out of the boat and tie her up. Riley turns and looks straight at me and then I realise what it is.

They have given in to Ivan's demands. This is to be his boat. I stand up, my heart thumping, watching the rocky foreshore and the stone walls of the barracks.

They must have been watching too because the five of them soon appear and I see Anton's fair head amongst them.

As they approach the jetty Riley Allen and the other men retreat. Anton struggles to be free of Karl's grasp but it isn't until the boys reach the boat that they let him go.

"Anton!" I yell. His face breaks into a grin and I watch as he runs towards me, loving him, so elated that I feel I'm going to burst. We fling our arms around each other and it feels so good. Then we climb up the gangplank together.

We join Grigori and Boris at the rail in time to watch Ivan and friends pull away from the jetty. I can tell they haven't had much experience with boats before, their rowing is awkward and uneven and they have trouble going in a straight line.

"Come on, Ivan, put some muscle into it!" yells Grigori.

He looks up and when he sees us watching he scowls and shouts something to Karl, who is rowing beside him. They begin to make some headway.

When they have gone about a hundred yards, the boat seems to come to a sudden stop as if it has hit an invisible wall.

Then we see it. A long rope is attached to the boat underwater and to the jetty. Riley, Burl and two other men sprint back to the jetty and begin hauling them in like fish.

We laugh until our sides ache. The four boys look at first astonished and then angry and then helpless, looking for a means of escape, but there is none, except jumping into the sea. And then what?

They are each grabbed and dragged ashore and then forcibly marched up the gangplank onto the *Yomei Maru*. Burl loops their numbered discs round their necks like nooses. I hope they are locked in somewhere until we sail. Iron shackles would be best.

I take back what I thought about Riley Allen. What he wants, he gets.

I haven't laughed so much for a long time. Not since we had a family photo taken and father got impatient with waiting for the long exposure time and he said something. Then the shutter snapped. He really spoilt that photo with his mouth open and his brows bunched together in a frown, but we always laugh when we look at it.

I get that from him. His impatience.

Chapter 12

We leave Vladivostok at five a.m. on July 14th 1920 and many of us come up on deck to say farewell to our homeland, although for me this far eastern corner of Siberia does not seem much like home.

Two days later, I turn sixteen.

That is the day we stop in Muroran in Japan. A lot of Japanese workmen come aboard to fix a plumbing problem in the girls' washroom so most of us go ashore and visit a couple of schools. The children put on a gymnastic display for us and I am impressed. Some of our girls sing some Russian songs in return. It's a good day. I know Anton is enjoying it. He seems all right after his ordeal with Ivan.

We settle in well to shipboard life. We are all impressed at how well the ship has been fitted out to accommodate us. The holds have been converted into giant dormitories with triple metal bunks. Grigori, Anton and I share one with Anton on the bottom bunk although he doesn't like that. He thinks we are treating him like a baby so I promise to swap later on. I have the middle one.

Bathrooms have been constructed on the decks, starboard side for boys and portside for girls, and then there are the big canvas sails directing wind into the holds and two enormous fans to get rid of the stale air. It's a wonderful invention.

The Red Cross staff have their own small cabins which have been constructed on the deck, and there is even a hospital.

A schedule has been arranged, probably by Miss Stepovich.

Tables and chairs have been set out on deck and we have breakfast just after seven. Then Burl Bramhall inspects our beds and after that there is school which lasts until noon. We have dinner in several sittings and later in the afternoon we have games and exercise.

Everyone has their jobs to do and as well as everyday jobs some of us work too. I am in charge of the food stores again like on Russian Island in Vladivostok. I like that job because I can do it on my own.

After tea at six o'clock we have time to ourselves and lights out is at nine-thirty. Grigori and I complained about that to Miss Stepovich but she says it's impossible to change it, since we are all ages in the holds and the little ones need their sleep.

Ivan and his three friends are refusing to do any work or lessons and I think in the end Riley Allen has given up. At least they are on board, and that's all that matters to him.

It's strange being surrounded by sea without any land in sight. The first days are warm and sunny and the sea calm. It seems about as different from home as I can imagine, and that makes me more homesick. Every day takes us further away, yet every day takes us nearer too. That is the one thought in my mind.

It gets very hot in the holds and we look forward to our time on deck, even though there isn't a lot of clear deck space, what with the extra structures and coal heap. Some of the crew got really mad with us and shouted in Japanese and the next day Riley Allen said he had agreed with the captain that we should alternate decks each day, one day port side and the next starboard side to give the crew room to work.

Every Saturday night a dance is held and Tatiana is teaching me to foxtrot. She's good and I tell her again that she ought to learn ballet.

"I can't understand how you can do ballet and not ballroom," she says.

"I can, I can waltz."

We are well matched. She has grown taller but so have I. Once we found that everyone had moved back to form a circle and watch us and we swept round the floor unimpeded by others. It felt so good to dance again. At the end everyone clapped and whistled and then suddenly the music changed to Russian folk and we clapped and stamped with lumps in our throats thinking of our homeland far away.

Boris tries to outdo his father with the Cossack kicks but only manages five seconds and we tease him about it all the time.

"It takes lots of practice," he keeps saying, defensively. "And where can I practice here?"

It's true. Space is far too limited. He'd be liable to kick someone in the shins. And there are some whom I would enjoy seeing that happen to.

One evening Tatiana drags me outside after we have finished the dance.

"I want to tell you something," she says, giggling.

We sit under a lifeboat sheltered from the cool wind.

"It's Riley and Miss Stepovich," she says. "I saw them kissing!" I can feel her hot breath against my cheek and her voice shakes a little with excitement. "Do you think they're in love?"

"When?" I ask. "When did you see them?"

"Earlier. I had to go to the bathroom and I was walking back when I heard some whispering and went to look. They didn't see me."

"How did you know it was them? It's dark."

I felt her sigh with exasperation. "There was a lamp nearby. I could see their silhouettes. It *was* them!"

"Well, they need a bit of fun too," I say. I'm bored and want to get back to the dance. I'm getting cold too, and begin to stand up.

"Wait!" Tatiana grabs my arm and pulls me back down onto the crate we are sitting on. "Nikolai... I've read about people having shipboard romances. Do you think it would be fun?" I know her face is really close now. Her breaths are rapid and hit my face in warm little blasts. Her hand searches for mine.

"No!" I pull away from her rather more violently than I intend. The thought terrifies me. Romance? I'm not ready for romance. Things are complicated enough.

She catches her breath in a sort of sob, gets up and I hear her shoes clattering across the wooden deck even before I can move. Now I've hurt her feelings. I just don't understand girls.

She seems to avoid me for a while and I'm sad to lose her friendship. It felt good to have a girl for a friend and she's intelligent and interesting to talk to. She never mentions her parents much, they are both doctors and she didn't see much of them. She used to spend most of her time with her aunt who seemed to resent the extra burden.

Whenever our paths do cross, she puts that elegant chin of hers in the air and turns her head. Once I saw her talking to Ivan and she was smiling. Traitor!

Ivan and Karl and friends continue their arrogant loud-mouthed criticism of everything the Red Cross do for us. Most of us are so used to that and we hardly take any notice but when it's personal it's difficult to ignore. I am sick of their name-calling. They seem to think of new ways of getting at me each time they see me – and that's almost every day.

"Don't get angry, Nikolai. It only encourages them." Now it's Anton giving *me* advice!

"I'm not."

"You are! You can't hide how you feel, it shows on your face."

I try not to think about Ivan and look forward to arriving in San Francisco. We are due to dock tomorrow and there's tremendous excitement on the ship already. We've been at sea for two weeks.

Lifeboat drill today is at three o'clock and we all assemble at our stations with our lifebelts on, used to the routine now. The boys are assigned to the twenty-three rafts and the girls to the twelve boats.

Riley Allen inspects us and Ivan and Karl have not bothered to turn up as usual. Two Red Cross workers are sent to find them and they finally appear with the usual sneering grins on their faces.

"Where are your lifebelts?" asks Riley.

The boys shrug.

"If," says Riley, "this ship should be unfortunate enough to sink, you four will not know the drill. It's for your own good that we rehearse in case of the unexpected."

"Oh, don't you worry," says Karl, "we'd know what to do. We'd be first in a lifeboat."

"Raft," corrects Riley. "That's what I mean."

"No, boat," says Ivan. "We wouldn't risk our lives in one of those flimsy things."

"The boats are for the girls and women."

The boys grin and look at each other. "Better and better," says Karl.

We all look at Riley to see what he's going to do next. His face looks like a boiler about to blow. Burl Bramhall strolls over, having seen the whole thing.

"Tomorrow we arrive in San Francisco," he says. "Unless you attend life boat drill in the morning, you will not be allowed ashore, and to make sure, we will lock you in the brig."

We all know what that is. It was built on the poop deck and looks like a log cabin with windows high up and it is escape-proof. The heavy door is locked with a large padlock. So far no-one has occupied it.

I see a shadow of apprehension briefly cross Karl's face but the others just shrug again and we are all dismissed and begin to untie our lifebelts.

Riley and Burl walk away.

"Hey! Why don't you leave that on, Nikolai?" says Ivan. "You could dance in it. That and your tights. You could pretend you were a real man, then, with real muscles."

Karl laughs. "Do you think he's got hairs on that puny chest of his?"

"I doubt it. Do girls have hairs on their chest?"

"Not usually."

Ivan is standing on an iron bollard half sitting on the rail, and Karl sits beside him, their heads thrown back as they laugh loudly.

I have had enough. I leap forward, drawing back my right fist as I go, and then give it to him, right on that laughing mouth. That will shut him up. It doesn't do my fingers much good though, and hurts like hell, but how I enjoyed it!.

Ivan looks astonished at first. He certainly hadn't seen it coming, hadn't thought for a moment that I had it in me. Blood begins to dribble down the side of his mouth. Then as we all watch, he begins to tip backwards. The look of astonishment turns to one of fear. He reaches out to grasp something and for a moment appears to regain his balance as his fingers clutch the rail. A look of relief slowly spreads over his face and his mouth relaxes in the beginnings of a smile.

At that moment the bows of the ship dip into a trough and Ivan's expression changes again to fear as he realises he is losing his balance. Then he is gone. Tipped backwards into the sea. Everyone hears the scream – and the splash.

No-one does anything. For a long time nobody moves. Then someone shouts "Man overboard!" and I spring to the side of the ship and fling myself after Ivan into the sea.

Chapter 13

It's a long way down to the water and it stings as I slap into it. Cold too. Very cold.

Because of my lifebelt I don't go under very far but although the sea looks calm enough from aboard the ship, from down here there is quite a swell so that I can't see more than a few yards in any direction.

I don't really know what made me leap in after him but I felt responsible in a way, since it had been my fist that had knocked him overboard. I hate him but I don't want him to drown. Also I have a vague recollection of someone saying he can't swim.

I can feel my clothes dragging me down and wonder if I'd still have jumped in if I hadn't been wearing my lifebelt.

I turn this way and that but still can't see Ivan.

There's a blast from the ship's whistle for some reason and I hope it's because someone has notified the captain and she has stopped.

Then I hear Ivan and the next second his terrified face appears on top of a wave. He's flailing his arms around in a panic.

"I can't swim! Help me!" His head goes under again and I swim towards him, wondering how on earth I am going to be able to save him. I'm not a strong swimmer but I have the advantage of the lifebelt and I reach out to him but as I do so one of his arms strikes me on the side of the face, knocking me under. I take in a mouthful of water and can't breath. I'm on the verge of panic. He's going to drown us both. Then I cough and spew out the seawater.

"Keep still!" I splutter.

I hear more splashing and Riley Allen appears and we each grab one of Ivan's arms and begin to swim towards the ship. She's some distance away, having obviously taken time to stop but one of her dinghies has been launched and two of the crew are rowing steadily towards us. I can see them now and again as they reach the crest of a wave.

Ivan is still yelling and struggling and making a complete fool of himself and I can't help smiling. Oh revenge is sweet!

They've let down a rope ladder for us to climb up and I'm very cold by now and can't control my shivering. My hands are almost numb and I'm having trouble grasping the rungs and hauling myself up the moving side of the ship. Hands reach out from the top and pull me aboard and Miss Stepovich throws a blanket round me. When Ivan finally comes aboard I see him shrug off the offered blanket and stagger away, presumably to his bunk.

I don't see him again for the rest of the day but now it's our final lifeboat drill before our arrival in San Francisco later today. He is here, as are the other three, all wearing their lifebelts. His face is sullen probably to disguise his humiliation. He doesn't look at me nor does he thank me for saving his life, but I don't expect it from him. Riley Allen comes to inspect us again and acts completely normally, checking each of us off the list, and never making any special reference to Ivan's presence. I doubt he will get any thanks either.

The captain is not pleased. In fact someone overheard he and Riley Allen having a terrific row and reported it to me. The captain has ordered Riley to keep us under control and I think that's ironic coming from a captain who has little control of his crew.

I could have enjoyed Ivan's discomfort for a little longer but our arrival in San Francisco overshadows that incident.

Everyone crowds along the rails as we enter the harbour. On the left is a rocky Island with a fort and a lighthouse. Riley tells us it's Alcatraz Island and was built as a military prison but now houses civilian prisoners. No-one can escape because the sea is so cold and there are dangerous currents. It looks like a really menacing place.

Then we sail through a narrow channel which he tells us is called Golden Gate, into San Francisco Bay and our first glimpse of the city.

We are all speechless. The whole mass of us there on deck gazes in silence at the panorama unfolding in front of us. Then eight hundred voices rise in excited chatter.

It really is a stunning sight. The city is built on hills and the buildings look as white as if they've been specially cleaned in our honour.

As we near our berth at the quay we can see an enormous crowd of people who begin to wave as we draw nearer.

"Are they waiting for us?" asks Anton with awe in his voice.

I nod. "Yes. I think they are."

The grey mass of people begins to take on individual features as we edge alongside the wharf and the great ropes are flung over the mooring bollards. I scan the faces with a mixture of surprise and apprehension. There is something overwhelming about being the object of welcome from people we don't know.

We disembark, in numerical order as usual, which means that Anton and I are among the first to step ashore. That too is strange, as the ground seems to roll a little after being on the ship for so long.

Burl told us about the great earthquake they had here in 1906 and I think maybe they are having another just for us.

People smile and greet us in Russian and some push forward to hand us gifts as we pass. A long line of buses awaits us. We are going to be housed at Fort Winfield Scott which turns out to be in a very strategic position overlooking the Golden Gate entrance to the harbour.

As we arrive there another crowd awaits us – this time the Junior Red Cross, and they give us candy and gifts, toys to the younger ones. I get a book but it's in English. I'll learn to read it one day. When I show it to Miss Stepovich later she says it's called *The Adventures of Huckleberry Finn*.

Anton jumps up and down on his bed. "A real bed!" he says. "Look Nikolai." He jumps off the bed, sits down on it and opens a bag. "Look at all this candy! And I got a toy train engine, what did you get?"

There's a sort of manic excitement as if he doesn't know what to do first. Probably because of being cooped up on that crowded ship. Suddenly now there is lots of space and he is like a freed animal. I know how he feels.

"I got a book." I hold it up.

He frowns at the words on the front. Then he dismisses it with a shake of his head, absorbed again in his own bag of goodies. People have been so generous.

Through the window I can see a long line of children crossing the open space in front of the building. The last of the buses is just pulling away. It's a warm sunny day and in the distance I can see a strip of blue water.

We were the first to arrive in this dormitory and I chose a bed by a window. Now the door opens and it's Tatiana and three other girls.

"Oh, sorry," she says.

I shrug and smile. "Boys' dormitory."

She nods and smiles back. It's the first time we have had any contact since that night during the dance.

The girls back out of the door but before they can close it, several boys push past and come in.

"We're going to a park tomorrow," says one. "Miss Stepovich just told us. Did you know? "

"A park!" says Anton. "What fun."

Boris has come in and dumped his belongings on the bed next to mine the other side from Anton's. "Riley Allen says it's huge," he says. "There are lots of lakes where we can hire a boat and it's all built on sand near the beach. There are two windmills to pump water from a well to irrigate the hundreds of trees."

How he got so much information in such a short time amazes me and I am prepared to hear a lot more statistics about the park in the next couple of days.

Boris takes a breath.

"Let's go and look around," I say quickly, and we go outside, the three of us. I know just how Anton feels. I have an urge to run so I do. I just set off and tear across the grounds, my feet flying over the grass. It feels wonderful.

"There's the sea. It's where we came in," says Anton as we reach a headland. It's a spectacular sight. Opposite is the other peninsular forming the Golden Gate and to our right the vast bay with the city sprawling across the hills.

We spend the whole of the next day at Golden Gate Park. It's huge. Lots of trees and lakes and a children's playground with a carousel. There's a conservatory full of plants for anyone who's interested. Not me. I like the lakes best and we have fun rowing around. Strange that we should want to go back on water again but this is different. I'll be surprised if we see Ivan on the water though!

There are lots of birds here, peacocks and pheasants and also deer and some funny looking creatures called moose with great big flat antlers and big noses. I hear that there are kangaroos too but I don't see any. Maybe it's a joke.

Anton has gone off for a donkey ride and I am sitting down by one of the bigger lakes throwing stones into the water and watching them skim and bounce over the surface.

"I can do four bounces," says a voice. It's Tatiana, and she sits down beside me.

"Show me," I say, pleased that we're talking again.

She does a two and then a three. I laugh.

"I can," she insists. "You're putting me off."

We both laugh and lie back with the sun warm on our faces. I feel comfortable with her again. She has forgiven me and I'm surprised at how important that is.

"Why do you think they're doing all this for us?" she asks. "I mean, it must be costing a lot of money."

"That's what the Red Cross does," I say. "Helps people."

She sits up on one elbow. "Yes, but the American Red Cross helping Russian children?"

I shrug.

"Do you like Riley Allen?"

"Of course. I admire him too. He gets what he wants. He doesn't give in."

"And Burl Bramhall?"

"I like him too." I open one eye and look at her. She blushes.

I grin. "Are you sweet on Burl? He's too old for you."

"No, he isn't," she retorts, answering my question. "He's only twenty-eight."

"And you are fifteen?"

She ignores that and says, "He's so quiet and calm even in a crisis. He has a good sense of humour – and such nice eyes."

"And those are the things you like in a man?"

She thinks for a minute, tilting her head sideways. "Yes."

"Does he feel the same about you?"

"He danced with me three times at the last dance," she says. "He complimented me on the way I looked. His Russian is really good now."

"I'm learning English," I say, wanting to change the subject. "Miss Stepovich says I have a good accent."

"It's not going to much use in Russia," she says, sitting up and plucking at some grass. "Especially for you as a ballet dancer. It's French you need, isn't it?"

Anton arrives back smelling of donkey.

"What are you two talking about?" he asks mischievously, his twinkly eyes darting from one of us to the other.

"French," I say, scrambling to my feet. "Want another boat ride?"

The three of us climb into the small rowing boat and push away from the shore. Sun glints on the water and I can smell the trees. For the moment there is no sound except for an automobile chugging along a nearby road. I think it's a shame that they allow them in the park.

I want to store this day in my memory so that I can bring it out and experience it again when we are on the ship. There is such a long way to go yet.

Maybe I will need this memory even when we are back in Russia again too.

Chapter 14

On 5th August we leave San Francisco with an even greater crowd seeing us off than had welcomed our arrival. A band plays too, and keeps on playing until we can't hear it any more. Just the odd note comes to us and we strain our ears to catch them.

Back past Alcatraz and out to sea. Then we turn south. There is quite a swell and the ship rises and falls taking people off guard sometimes. Miss Stepovich organises lessons for the younger ones while we go about our duties.

"Can't I help you?" asks Anton, frowning at the classes assembling. "I don't feel like lessons."

I can understand his reluctance. I think we all feel the same. It's difficult to get back to doing normal things after our stay in San Francisco. It's been the experience of a lifetime. A place none of us could have imagined. There is so much to think about that trying to turn our minds to math and science is almost impossible. What kindness we found there.

"Go on," I say. "Miss Stepovich looks sad. See if you can make her laugh."

He turns to look at the teacher. "Why is she sad? Doesn't she want to leave San Francisco either?"

"No," I say. But I know the real reason. Riley Allen is not on board. He has gone to Washington to the Red Cross headquarters. He hinted that there was a problem he has to sort out but I have confidence that we have nothing to worry about.

But Miss Stepovich is missing him.

I grin at Anton and give him a little push. "Go one," I say "I'll see you later." I must be careful or I'll get like Tatiana.

As the weather becomes hotter the atmosphere aboard the ship changes. It's August and we are heading south towards the Panama Canal. Soon it becomes so hot that games and exercise are stopped and eventually lessons too. We don't know what to do all day. Boris is one of several people who get heatstroke and has to go to the hospital and be packed in ice to reduce his temperature. He'd been complaining of a bad headache and dizziness and felt sick. He looked awful when I saw him just before he went to the hospital and only seemed half conscious. It's frightening and we wonder who will be next.

Miss Stepovich is ill too.

The crew is not immune to the heat either and every afternoon between two and three-thirty, the ship's engines are stopped to allow the engineers to come out on deck and the engines to cool a little.

One of the boys went completely demented and threatened to jump overboard so has to have a guard at all times.

At night the holds are stifling and when someone suggests we take our beds up on deck to sleep the idea soon catches on and many of us pick up our pillows and mattresses and haul them out onto the deck. There's a slight breeze which feels wonderful.

Anton and I go up front on the starboard bow and throw down our mattresses and pillows, claiming our space. I lie down, gaze up at the stars and take some deep breaths of fresh air. Anton giggles and I turn to him and grin.

Soon there is no space left and we all begin to settle down to a good night's sleep.

One of the teachers comes out. "There is not enough room on the decks for everyone," she says. "Sorry boys, but back you go. I know it's hot but it's not fair if only some can sleep out here."

All right for her, I think. She has a cabin built on the deck. *They* don't have to sleep with two hundred others in a windowless airless pit. Even Burl's canvas sail isn't helping much now..

I sit staring after her and then get up and snatch up my pillow and mattress. Give me the cold anytime.

A rumble of dissent is spreading around the deck. Those who have a place are not giving it up easily and those who haven't are still trying to push people aside to make space.

The teacher turns back. "Now!" she says.

Still many, me included, stalls for time. Someone starts a chant.

"We won't go back! We won't go back!"

I join in and Anton, looking up at my face for guidance, starts shouting too. It's time *we* had a say about something. We could take it in turns to sleep on deck, couldn't we? At least those down below would have more space too.

Then a boy without a space on the deck whacks another boy with a pillow and in a moment pillows and feathers are flying everywhere until the deck looks like a slaughter on a chicken farm. It reminds me of the chicken I crushed to death and I start to fight my way back to the hatch with my mattress and pillow intact. I've had enough.

There's a splash and I look back. If anyone's fallen overboard I'm not going to jump in after them this time. But it is bedding being flung overboard in protest. There are going to be some uncomfortable nights ahead for some.

Not only have all the Red Cross people been woken by the noise but the Captain and crew have too. The captain is dancing about shaking his fists and I suddenly want to laugh. Poor Burl, that most placid person, is trying to calm everything down.

Behind the ship a wake of bedding bobs in a long white line and I wonder what other ships might make of it.

Anton and I go back down into the hold and listen as the chaos above slowly abates.

"Nikolai," says Anton.

I look over the edge of my bunk. He is smiling. "It was fun, wasn't it?"

I nod. What a responsibility it is having a younger brother. I am supposed to lead a good example, aren't I?

I peer over the bunk again. "Anton?" He has his back to me and he turns back over to face me.

"Tomorrow we'll change bunks. You can come up here if you like."

He smiles and nods and then curls up for sleep.

The next day there is a storm. It is short and sharp with rain heavier than I've ever seen, and it is over in half an hour but takes a lot of the heat with it and washes the decks leaving little heaps of sodden feathers as a reminder of the previous night's skirmish. The extra work makes the crew angrier than they already are and they spit out torrents of Japanese if we go within earshot.

Our passage through the Panama Canal provides a diversion and for the whole fifty mile journey there is hardly ever a time when the rails are not filled with people watching the locks fill and empty or waving to anyone on the shore.

Boris is better and has been discharged from hospital with instructions to stay in the shade but he is determined not to miss this event.

"About 28,000 men died during the construction," he says, as the four of us lean over to watch the ship sinking in the lock. I know we are in for the statistics again and groan.

"Yes?"

"Accidents and Yellow Fever and things," he goes on, "landslides too."

It's a staggering thought.

"It was finished in 1914," he continues, "otherwise we would have had to go an extra eight thousand miles…"

"Shut up, know-all," says a familiar voice behind, and for once I welcome Ivan's interruption. I haven't seen much of him for a long time. He seems to be keeping his head down since the fall overboard.

Boris looks miffed and closes his mouth.

We watch in silence as the enormous gates open and hear the churning of the propellers as we prepare to move forward out of the lock.

I think of what Boris said. Twenty-eight thousand men dying to build this thing. Futile. Like wars.

Miss Stepovich is still ill and every day the nurses report her condition to us at breakfast. At first there were always crowds of children milling round the hospital at most times of day, asking after her and hampering the nurses' work, so they have started this daily bulletin. They reassure us that it isn't serious. An infection of the bone near her ear, they say. It has a name but I've forgotten it.

Our arrival in New York on 28th August 1920 is not the joyous occasion it would have been because, as we dock at the quay in New Jersey, an ambulance is waiting and two orderlies come aboard to carry Miss Stepovich ashore by stretcher.

As they bring her out of the hospital some of the younger children surge forward calling to her, and have to restrained by Red Cross people. Miss Stepovich waves and smiles but her face is pale and she has aged so much.

bearers negotiate the gangplank I see him start forward out of the crowd which have gathered to meet us. He springs onto the gangplank and I can see that his eyes are only for her. Some people call out to him and wave but he appears not to hear, and, as the stretcher reaches the quay, he grasps her outstretched hand and bends over her. She is loaded into the ambulance, and it is only then that he seems to realise where his duty lies. He cannot go with her to the hospital but has to take over responsibility for us again.

"Poor Riley." Tatiana is beside us.

"He could have gone with her," I say. "We could manage without him for a bit longer."

"No," says Tatiana. "His work must come first."

She surprises me sometimes. I thought her head was full of romance and here she is adamant about where duty lies.

He is coming up the gangplank now, waving and smiling and when he reaches the top he gathers several children into his arms.

"How I've missed you," he says, and I smile because I know he means it.

We leave the ship and climb aboard three smaller United States Army steamers to be taken to our accommodation. It's another fort – Fort Wadsworth, and is on a big island called Staten Island, and again the fort guards the entrance to the harbour. On the top of one building is a lighthouse to guide ships. The view is spectacular.

The next day is Sunday and church services are held outside with the help of the choir from St. Nicholas' Cathedral. The weather is fine and warm and this afternoon people start arriving on the ferry from the city. Hundreds and hundreds of people, mostly Russian immigrants.

Grigori, Boris, Anton and I go for a long walk around the grounds after the service and as we walk back the people run towards us, greeting us in our language and handing us candy and gifts again. It's overwhelming. I've never said thank you so many times.

Then two men come up to us. They are not smiling and have no gifts.

"What do you think about being sent to France, the enemy of our country?" one says.

I stare at him. It's the first we've heard about it.

"Ha! They haven't told you," he says. "Because when you get there you will be forced to join the military and sent to the Polish front to fight against our own country."

"No," says Grigori, "I don't believe they would do that."

The second man waves his arm around to indicate where we are. "What do you think about being kept imprisoned on this island? It is a disgrace."

I shake my head. "It isn't true! An army fort is the obvious place to accommodate such a large number. The American Red Cross have looked after us well."

"No-one does these things for nothing. Don't be naïve, boy! There is always an ulterior motive."

I want to ask why they are living here, then, since it's such a bad place, but they move off to speak to others. I don't believe them but it does sow a small seed of suspicion in my mind.

We four look at each other.

"I don't believe it," says Boris. "Riley Allen would never send us to an enemy country."

"Maybe he doesn't have the last word," says Grigori. "He doesn't hold a high position in the American Red Cross. Remember he said he was a newspaper editor in Hawaii, who volunteered to help in Europe. He was just the Press Officer."

That night there is a lot of excited talk amongst we older ones.

"We have to protest somehow," says Alexei. He was one of those who spoke to the teachers all that time ago in Koure.

"But how do we know it's true?" asks Grigori. "Who were those men?"

"They were supporters of our new government," says Alexei. "They are our people, our fellow countrymen. Don't you believe them over these Americans? You have forgotten who you are, Grigori. If you are a good Russian you are a supporter of our great Lenin and the Russian Communist Party."

I'm confused. We have been away so long that we only hear fragments of what is going on at home in Russia and I don't really understand much.

Tatiana is up there too. "You heard what they said would happen to us if we are sent to France," she says. "The older boys will be conscripted into the army, the girls put into prostitution and the little ones held hostage. We cannot risk this happening. We must put our thoughts in writing," she says. "Say we refuse to go. They can't force us all."

So a paper is drawn up and we all sign it, about two hundred of us anyway, and Tatiana solemnly takes it to Riley Allen's room. In it we demand that the American Red Cross changes its decision to send us to France.

Riley Allen acknowledges the protest by saying that he will do what he can. For the next few days we see little of him and when we do, he looks tired and worried. I think of what Tatiana said about him leaving his job and volunteering to help people in Europe who were in a dire situation as a result of war – and he's ended up with us. How could any man cope with such responsibility? And he has Miss Stepovich to worry about too.

The big highlight of our stay in New York, we are told, is to be a concert in a place called Madison Square Garden.

We are taken there by a fleet of buses and as Anton and I step out of ours a man with a camera pushes into our column and speaks to me in Russian.

"Hello, I'm from the New York Times," he says. "What do you think about Riley Allen being dismissed?"

I am stunned and it must show on my face. He holds his camera up and there's a crack and a blinding light. Then he pushes a card into my hand and disappears back into the crowd.

I look around at the concerned faces who have overheard the reporter. "Did you hear that? They can't dismiss Riley."

Tatiana pushes through to us. "Who was that? What did he say?"

She goes pale when I tell her. Despite being strongly against going to France, I know she likes and admires Riley.

"What's going on?" It's Burl Bramhall. "Who was that, Nikolai?"

"A reporter from the New York Times." Tatiana answers for me, straightening her elegant back and looking up at Burl with a smile, despite the serious situation.

"Nikolai will have his photo in the paper tomorrow."

"What's this about Riley being dismissed?" I ask.

Burl shakes his head. "Just keep moving. You're holding things up."

I look at the card the reporter gave me. Tom Minsky. I shove it into my pocket.

Madison Square Garden is a huge building with columned archways and a high tower on top. Inside is an enormous hall – the largest in the world Burl tells us, with seating for eight thousand people, and as we enter it seems as if it is almost full. A great cheer goes up as we troop down the aisle and take our seats in the front rows reserved for us.

A Russian Orchestra plays first and then the stage darkens and three balalaika players come on and play a selection of Russian folk music which have the audience cheering and shouting for more. The New York audience, that is.

We are quiet and I can hear someone behind me crying. It is a time for remembering our families back in Petrograd and wondering how they are. It's months since we had any news.

Is mother all right, all alone? How is she coping? Without us and without father. I took them for granted, after all, they were always there, the two of them.

For the first time I think about their marriage. We heard about how they met – my mother tripped over father's feet getting off a bus. They were always laughing. Thinking back now I can remember how they used to look at each other, although it meant nothing to me at the time.

I realise now that they certainly loved each other very much.

Now my mother has lost him – and she may think we are lost too. But she sent us away from the appalling deprivation of the city to give us a chance. How difficult that decision must have been for her, and she had to make it alone.

I come back to the present. The balalaika players have left the stage and the stage lights have gone up. A man walks on and takes up a position in the middle of the stage. He is tall and slim with dark hair and a moustache and he isn't smiling.

"Ladies and gentlemen and children of the Petrograd Colony," he begins, "my name is Artur Popov and I am a representative of the Soviet Bureau."

I hear a murmur from the large crowd behind and people shuffle in their seats as they strain to hear.

The man begins to criticise the American Red Cross saying that it is not the neutral organisation it pretends to be. He says they have political motives and that they have kidnapped us and are holding us in prison camps, intent on sending us to an enemy country – France.

The audience begins to respond to his words when he speaks of us being hostages in a conspiracy against the Motherland. They are very emotional words and evoke more and more reaction from the audience.

I look round and many are standing and shouting, arms punching the air in outrage at his words. Several policemen stand at one of the entrances and I think I can see Riley Allen. I look round to see where our nearest exit is in case it gets really dangerous. The people are on our side but some of us could get hurt if it reached riot proportions. Many of the younger children are crying and being comforted by our teachers.

I feel Anton's hand creep into mine – something he hasn't done for a long time. He tugs at my hand to get my attention.

"What's happening?"

"This man is spoiling everything," I say. "It is all lies."

As I speak I feel a surge of anger rise up to support my words. Strength comes with it, and conviction. It's an overwhelming fierce rage which brings tears to my eyes yet I feel words erupting into my mouth. Words which have to be spoken.

Shaking Anton's fingers from mine, I stand up and run to the stage steps, mounting them two at a time.

"You are wrong!" I shout. "It is all lies."

The spotlight swings onto my face, blinding me for a moment. I run towards the man. He has stopped talking and is looking at me with eyebrows drawn in an angry frown.

I have caught him by surprise and he is slow to respond. Then I turn to the audience, just a vast hazy blur. They are sitting down again and are almost instantly quiet.

The words pour out as if they have a life of their own. I don't have to think, they just come. I tell them of how the civil war cut us off from the west. We could not get back to Petrograd and were starving and freezing with only our summer clothes. Our teachers did everything they could for us but still we had had to resort to stealing for survival.

Then when things were at their worst and we no longer had the strength to steal or even crawl out of our pile of rags we called our beds, along had come Riley Allen, like Santa Claus, on Christmas Eve.

There is not a sound in the auditorium. I am aware that Artur Popov has crept forward again but a growl from the audience sends him back into the wings.

Someone else has stepped onto it. I pause near the end of my story and turn to see Tatiana there. She smiles at me and comes forward.

In that pause I hear Ivan's voice and Alexei's too shouting against Riley, but we ignore them.

Tatiana backs up everything I have said but adds that, much as we owe the American Red Cross, we are *opposed* to being sent to France.

I finish with a plea that Riley Allen not be sacked, and we leave the stage together, to a tumultuous applause.

The Colony is split. Many believe and agree with Artur Popov yet most remain loyal to Riley Allen and the ARC. There are some noisy arguments in the barracks long into the night.

Tatiana pulls me outside for some fresh air. It's hot and I am losing my voice with all the shouting. I'm exhausted but proud of myself. I wonder if that reporter got a better photograph of me to replace the first.

A cool breeze blows in off the sea and we stroll round keeping fairly close to the buildings. I feel her hand reach for mine and it feels very different to Anton's. At that moment I know that I have suddenly grown up. I am no longer a boy.

As we pass a gap between two buildings, I draw Tatiana into the narrow alleyway and kiss her hard on the mouth. For a split second she resists and stiffens, then she relaxes and kisses me back.

When we break apart I say, "How do my kisses rate against Burl's?"

She is silent.

"He hasn't kissed you yet?" I tease.

In the darkness I see her shake her head. At least she is honest and I admire her for it. Most people would have lied.

We move slowly back into the open, her hand in mine again. We stand in silence watching the moon glinting on the ocean.

A light goes on nearby spoiling the effect and we turn to see that two people have entered a room behind us. The window is open and we instinctively dodge back so as not to be seen. Whoever it is would not be pleased to see us out here alone and we don't want to be put into an embarrassing position in front of all the others.

We start to move away but a voice I recognise speaks.

"You don't understand," he is saying, "surely you didn't think I meant it when I said we were taking the children home to their parents?" He laughs, something I hadn't heard him do before. But there is no humour in it.

"We shall take them back to Russia, of course," he continues, "but then we must keep them together in an orphanage. Now they have been exposed to a western capitalist society we cannot let them loose to spread any propaganda they may have picked up."

"But what about their parents?" The other man's voice seems familiar but I can't place it. Tatiana huddles closer to me as we listen.

"It's simple," says Artur Popov. "We tell the children that there parents are dead. Maybe they starved or were shot as dissenters, who cares? To the parents we shall say that the ship was lost at sea." He laughs again. "All gone at the same time. Poof! And don't worry, Victor, I promised I would see that the authorities know how much you have helped me."

Victor! One of our teachers.

I feel Tatiana's fingers squeeze mine and pull away. When there is no danger of us being heard, we run.

We have to find Riley Allen at once.

Chapter 15

We know which block the Red Cross personnel are housed in but have no idea which is Riley's room so we knock on the first door we come to.

One of the teachers opens it, still pushing her arms into the sleeves of her dressing gown, and stares out at us.

"What are you doing here? Is something wrong?"

"We need to speak to Riley Allen. It's urgent but we don't know which is his room."

She frowns and looks up the corridor. "I think it's the third or fourth door on the right," she says. "But can I help?"

I shake my head. "Thank you."

We run to the third door and knock. It isn't Riley who opens it but Burl, so we repeat our plea.

"He has gone to visit Miss Stepovich in hospital," he says. "He hopes they will discharge her tomorrow so she can sail with us. Can I help?"

I look at Tatiana and she nods. Burl invites us in and we tell him what we overheard. He covers his face with his hands.

"Oh God," he says. "I knew he couldn't be trusted but what can we do? They're firing Riley and putting Artur Popov in charge. The Red Cross will only be in a caring role then, under his orders."

"But now that we know what he really intends..." I say.

"I'm sorry, Nikolai, but he will deny it. It is your word against his and after you two standing up for us today, no-one is going to believe you. They'll think it's a ploy to discredit him."

He sighs. "Look, there's nothing we can do now. You two get to bed and I'll tell Riley as soon as he gets back. And thanks." He smiles but his face looks drawn.

We decide to tell Grigori and Boris about what we've overheard with the idea that four heads are better than one if we have to take things into our own hands and come up with a plan. When we try to make light of what we were doing out there in the first place, I see Boris flash Grigori a quick grin but they don't say anything.

It is the morning of departure and we are to start boarding the small army boats to be ferried back to the Yomei Maru at ten o'clock. Being numbers twenty-two and twenty-three, Anton and I are, of course, among the first as usual.

There is no sign of Riley at breakfast and I go to look for Burl. He looks even more worried than ever and at first will not answer my question about the whereabouts of Riley. At last he seems to make a decision.

"Please don't let anyone else know, but he didn't come back last night. We think he may have been… detained at Red Cross Headquarters so as not to cause a political rumpus."

I nod, my mind in a whirl. We have to think of something quickly. Who can help?

When I get back to the others Boris has a newspaper in his hand and he thrusts it in front of my face. "Front page. Look," he says.

There I am. Not looking stunned outside Madison Square Garden at the news that Riley was to be dismissed, but in full spate on the stage.

Then I have it! I know who to contact. The journalist of the New York Times!

I delve into my pocket and pull out the card.

"What do you think?" Boris is saying. "You're famous!"

I shake my head to dismiss his trivialities. "Listen! I'm not supposed to tell anyone but Riley didn't come back last night. Burl thinks the Red Cross are keeping him out of trouble until we leave."

"But they have to let him say goodbye," says Anton.

I grab his sleeve. "You mustn't talk to anyone about this, Anton. Promise? It's really important."

He nods. He wasn't there when Tatiana and I told Grigori and Boris about the overheard conversation. It's best he doesn't know about that.

I look at the clock in the hallway. It's nine o'clock. How am I going to contact the journalist? His card has a telephone number on it and there must be a telephone here in the fort, maybe more than one.

"I'm going to find a telephone," I say. "If I can speak to the journalist maybe he can do something."

The most obvious place for a telephone is in the Commanding Officer's office, I think, but I have no idea where that is. While everyone is assembling in the grounds I make my way to the administration building, hoping that no-one asks what I am doing.

I have to find a telephone although I have never used one before and my English is still poor. I will soon be missed. It doesn't take long for twenty-one people to board.

The first two doors I try are locked and I am beginning to despair when I have an idea. The room where we overheard Artur Popov talking may be open and may have a telephone. I quickly work out where it is from the outside geography. It is the last room in this building facing the ocean.

It is locked. I stand in the corridor with my head in a whirl. Our whole future depends on this. The future of everyone in the colony. If Riley Allen is not reinstated as leader and Artur Popov exposed, our fate will be sealed as soon as we leave United States' waters. I think of the overheard conversation and shudder. We would never see our mother again. She would be all alone, having lost her husband and then both her children.

The window! Have they remembered to close the window?

I speed out of the door and round the building and heave a huge sigh of relief when I see it is still open. To my right I can see children lining up in numerical order. No-one is looking this way but any second someone could raise the alarm without knowing they were destroying their own future.

I pull the window open as wide as it will go and haul myself the five feet or so off the ground. Then I'm in, my eyes scanning the room.

It is on the desk. I pull the journalist's card out of my pocket and look at the number as I sit at the desk and lift the earpiece. Then I dial the number and hear it ring at the other end.

"New York Times news desk," says a voice.

I rack my brains for some English but none comes so I just say his name.

"Tom Minsky, please."

"Hold on."

Another voice. "Minsky speaking."

"Hello. It's Nikolai here. From the Petrograd Children's colony. You took my photograph."

He laughs. "Yes, what do you think of it? Front page news!"

"Riley Allen is missing and something else has happened," I say, interrupting him. "The ship sails soon and we must find Riley. The future of everyone of us depends on it. Please believe me. I overheard the plan of what is really going to happen to us."

He didn't waste any words. "Can you get away? You must escape when you reach the quay on the mainland. I'll meet you there. In the meantime I'll try and find out where Riley Allen is."

"They think he is at Red Cross Headquarters," I say. "Just until we've sailed."

"I understand," he says, and hangs up.

I replace the earpiece and am out of the window and soon running to join the line of children waiting to board the army boat.

Anton has been holding my things. He looks relieved to see me.

"It's almost our turn, Nikolai. Where were you?"

"Never mind." I slot into the line. "When we get to the quay I'm going to escape." He looks alarmed. "I'll be back! I promise. I have to find Riley Allen. Make up something. Tell them I forget something or went to the toilet. Anything. You get on board the ship. All right?"

He nods dubiously.

"Anton, listen to me. Don't mention Riley Allen. I'll explain later but it is really important."

We board the steamer and as soon as it is full it leaves Staten Island to go across to mainland New Jersey where the Yomei Maru is waiting with steam up. As we dock I look around for a possible opportunity. There's a lot of cargo waiting to be loaded onto a ship and then a long stretch of open quay between that and our ship. That is it then. As soon as we step ashore I must duck behind the huge crates.

Anton grasps my hand and squeezes it then gives me a push. At the same time he lets out a yell, which almost has me turning back.

"I've hurt my ankle," he says, wincing.

I could hug him! In the diversion he causes I am soon behind the crates and making my way away from the quayside and back towards the road, feeling very conspicuous in my old hotchpotch of donated clothing.

There is no sign of Tom Minsky and I begin to wonder what I should do if he doesn't come. Maybe he didn't believe me and is just humouring me. What can I do? Stranded in New York illegally without any money.

Time goes by and I chance a look back towards the quay. Another wave of children is crowding up the gangplank of the Yomei Maru.

"Nikolai!"

I spin round and grin as I recognise Tom. He waves me to come over and I see that he has parked his automobile behind a warehouse.

"I've found Riley Allen," he says as we run. "You were right. He is at Red Cross Headquarters. I'm taking you there now so you can tell what you overheard. I can translate for you."

They are expecting us of course, and we are taken into a small office where Riley Allen and several others are waiting.

Riley smiles at me. "Hello Nikolai."

I run up to him and shake his hand. One of the other men speaks.

"They want you to tell them what you heard, Nikolai," says Tom, pointing to a chair for me to sit down.

So I tell them, and they look at each other alarmed. On Riley Allen's face there is an added hint of smugness and I catch his eye and we smile.

The man who seems to be in charge reaches for his telephone.

"They are telephoning the port authority," says Tom, "to try and stop the Yomei Maru from sailing."

I look at the clock on the wall. It is just after noon.

The man on the telephone hangs up, his face grave. Tom does not have to translate as I know what that means.

The ship has sailed.

Chapter 16

Riley springs from his chair as does the man at the desk. Tom grabs my arm. "Come on. They have asked the Harbour Master to stop the ship on some pretext. She has to comply otherwise she will be impounded."

The four of us get into an automobile and speed down towards the harbour and I hear the sound of a police car behind us. There is a harbour police boat waiting for us and we scramble aboard, one of the crew casting off at once.

As we move out into the harbour we can see the familiar shape of the Yomei Maru, her wake trailing out behind her.

"She's not stopping!" I say. We all hang onto the bows of the boat with eyes fixed on the stern of our ship which is defying the order to stop. Nevertheless we are faster than she is since she hasn't yet reached top speed and isn't a fast ship anyway.

The distance between us is slowly diminishing and as soon as we are within hailing distance, one of the policemen shouts through a megaphone.

We are close enough to see people crowding the stern rails now and some are waving. Faint calls come to us over the water.

The policeman again orders her to stop and I guess the captain has been following Artur Popov's orders but now takes command himself, afraid of having his ship impounded and maybe losing his captain's license. We are gaining more rapidly although the Yomei Maru's propellers are still idling, churning up the sea.

As we draw alongside there is some sort of skirmish on the deck but I can't see what is happening. After a few moments some of the crew let down the rope ladder. This is the second time I will be climbing this ladder and I hope it will be the last.

The police go first and I can see they are well practised. By the time I reach the deck followed by Tom, Riley Allen and the Red Cross man, the police have caught Artur Popov and the teacher, Victor. I recognise him now though have not had much to do with him.

It is just as well they can't understand what Artur Popov is shouting although they can probably guess. It is definitely anti-American and he is foolish enough to declare his intentions for us in the firm belief that it is the right thing to do.

Tom looks at me and shakes his head and for the first time I really wonder what life will be like at home in Russia now under the communist regime. Had anything been gained by the revolution or was it just an overturning of one bad system to be replaced by another? It is with mixed feelings that I look forward to getting home.

The good news is that Riley Allen is reinstated on the spot and a huge cheer goes up and I am the hero of the hour. The police leave with their two prisoners and Tom says goodbye.

"Keep in touch," he says as he disappears back down the ladder. I say I will. I couldn't have done it without him and what a story he will have to tell in his newspaper.

Another piece of good news is that Miss Stepovich has been discharged from hospital and is on board. Riley's face is all smiles when he hears about it.

As before we soon get back into the shipboard routine but it is hard after the excitement of the events in New York and everyone, despite the fiasco at Madison Square Garden and the decision to send us to France, has nothing but good to say about New York and the generosity of the people.

Riley told us that it still isn't certain exactly where we are going but he hopes we will soon receive some positive news. Since everyone now knows what Artur Popov really intended, despite his promise to take us home, even the most rebellious ones can do nothing but trust Riley.

Anton is taking part in a concert which has been hastily put together to cheer everyone up. Musical instruments were donated by Russian people in New York, and since he has had a few lessons on the guitar he was given one to play. Four or five rehearsals seems a little inadequate to me.

It's quite a cool evening, being the middle of September, but by no means cold as the audience assembles on deck for the concert. A ripple of pleasure sweeps through as Miss Stepovich appears, accompanied by Riley Allen, and they take seats in the front row. He wraps a blanket around her legs and she sits with her shawl round her shoulders, smiling and responding to people who speak to her.

The musicians troop out and sit down and we all wait expectantly. Grigori nudges me.

"How long does this last?"

I shrug, irritated. It hasn't started yet. Give them a chance.

The conductor, one of the teachers, comes out to great applause, holds up her arms, and the concert begins.

Well, some of the musicians begin, others are not quite ready, so the teacher begins again. The tunes which come out are recognisable, on the whole, but the tempo is very rocky and the harmonies often absent. I am beginning to agree with Grigori. We need to know how much longer we will have to endure the agony of discord.

The players' faces are tense with concentration and the conductor tries valiantly to keep it all going but is failing. The audience first begins to mutter amongst themselves and then one or two remarks are shouted out to the amusement of everyone else.

This derision gradually gets through to the musicians and I can't help but feel sorry for them as I watch the expression on their faces changing.

Someone else has seen it too.

Miss Stepovich flings off her blanket and gets unsteadily to her feet. Then she steps forward. I see Riley reach out to dissuade her but she goes first to have a word with the conductor, who nods and goes and sits down, then to the players. We all sit watching and wondering how she is going to save the situation as she seems to be showing them a note to play on their instruments.

She then takes the nearest balalaika after a word with its owner, sits down and begins to play.

The soft strains of *Kalinka* gradually grow into a frenzy of excitement while the musicians strum chords to accompany her. In the slower middle part each single delicate note seems to hang in the air and I hold my breath at the beauty of them. Then the tempo increases and soon we are all tapping our feet and a big cheer accompanies the final chord. Miss Stepovich follows that with *Dark Eyes* and more and as I look round, I see people weeping and singing and laughing at the same time. We are going home! After more than two years we are going back to our homeland.

When the concert ends there is an atmosphere of high emotion and joy and excitement. Miss Stepovich is surrounded by a swarm of children but Riley Allen soon whisks her away, his arm tenderly supporting her frail figure. Even from where I am I can see how tired she looks.

Anton is full of praise. "Wasn't she wonderful, Nikolai? We were awful but she saved the day. Doesn't she play well? When we get home I'm going to learn to play like that."

"You play the guitar."

He shakes his head vehemently. "No, I'm going to learn the balalaika. It's more traditional."

I laugh. I'm sure everyone will go to bed tonight full of hope for the future. Another week or so and we shall be arriving in Europe. We shall have done full circle.

Chapter 17

Miss Stepovich is dead.

It was more serious than we thought. Meningitis. No-one can believe it, especially when we remember her playing last night. She must have been feeling so ill then yet she played to save the musicians' embarrassment. That was typical of her.

The weather is bright and the sea calm but it is as if a heavy cloud has settled over the ship. The usual shouting and laughter are absent. No-one is running about or joking with each other or arguing or fighting. The normal sounds have been replaced by silence and whispers and tears.

I never knew such grieving was possible. It really makes me think about the importance one person can make, and the huge void left when they go. Suddenly you remember so many things about them that you took for granted when they were there and you begin to appreciate all the facets which make up a human being.

She was so well loved and respected by everyone and I know I will never hear a balalaika being played without thinking of her.

I am one of the last to hear the news. Having done my morning lessons I am in the food storage area just before twelve o'clock retrieving the necessary items for the evening meal and taking them to the galley.

Back on the main deck I am surprised to see that although the tables are laid for the first lunch sitting, no-one is there, where normally the younger children would already be scrambling to take their seats. Some of them know by now that I am in charge of the food stores and ask me what is for lunch.

The deck is quiet, the places all set and the corner of a tablecloth lifting silently in the breeze. The chairs stand neatly row on row on each side of the tables waiting for occupants.

Something is obviously wrong.

As I stand pondering and looking at the tables Anton appears and my heart sinks. His face has the same closed look as when we first started out on this trip, just after our father was killed.

"Nikolai." He is choked up and can hardly get the words out. "Miss Stepovich died this morning."

"What!" I am astounded. It is so unexpected, I thought she was getting better.

"Everyone is so…" he waves his arm behind him. "Everyone is crying. It's awful."

"What happened?"

"Riley was with her," he says. "She went into a coma and died at about six o'clock this morning."

I am speechless. It is so unfair. She had been so near to home and been through so much with us.

I can't think of anything else all day. I keep remembering how she threw off her blanket and went up to play because she couldn't stand to see the musicians laughed at. Not that the audience had meant to be cruel, most of them anyway, but she had been such a caring person that she hated seeing the musicians' miserable faces and had done something about it without thinking of herself. What an effort that must have been.

And Riley Allen. We don't see him at all day.

She is to be buried at sea tomorrow at noon.

Morning lessons have been cancelled and at eleven forty-five we all assemble on deck, all nine hundred or so of us as well as most of the crew. The weather is cloudy with a cool wind. Miss Stepovich's body lies on a board covered with a Red Cross flag. I stare at the inert shape and remember those soldiers shot by firing squad in Koure. I hope they had a proper burial or at least a few words said over them.

Four members of the Japanese crew, in their dress uniforms, stand by her body, one at each corner.

The ship's whistle sounds and the vibrations under my feet lessen and cease entirely as she stops engines. There is silence except for the canvas awnings by the hatches flapping in the wind, and the ship rocks gently on the light swell.

Riley Allen, accompanied by the captain, emerges from a doorway and the crowd of children part to let them through.

Riley has changed, I hardly recognise him. His face is bland and expressionless and pale and he staggers slightly as he walks through to stand beside Miss Stepovich's body. He doesn't look at it, in fact he doesn't seem to be looking at or seeing anything. We are standing quite close and I can see his face clearly.

The captain has a book in his hand and all eyes turn to him as he begins the burial service in Japanese. It seems a bit odd, but I suppose it is his duty.

All at once Riley holds up his hand and says something to the captain, who looks as though he is about to argue but thinks better of it. Riley reaches into his pocket and brings out a scrap of paper, then, in a voice which isn't much above a whisper, he begins to read.

"Remember me when I am gone away,

Gone far away into the silent land;
When you can no more hold me by the hand…"

Then he chokes, stops, swallows and begins again but he cannot read. I can see the tears pouring down his face and to see a man cry like that stuns me. I didn't know that love could be so great.

Burl steps forward, gently takes the paper from Riley's hand, and continues the poem. I can only understand parts of it but it must be beautiful.

A prayer is said in Russian and then the four crewmen lift the board on which Miss Stepovich lies and slowly carry it to the side of the ship where it rests on the rail for a moment. Then they tilt it up and from beneath the Red Cross flag her body slips into the sea.

I cannot see from where I am standing but I hear the splash and I can visualise it, wrapped in cloth, slowly sinking out of sight.

Many of the children are crying as are the teachers, her colleagues. I can't speak either and my eyes well up. I try to brush away the tears unobtrusively but Anton must have seen me, and been holding back like a man. Now he sees that it is all right to cry and he turns his face to my chest and weeps.

Slowly and silently the crowd disperses and the rumble under my feet starts up again as the ship gets underway. We have lost one passenger and things will never be the same again.

Riley Allen is at dinner that night but I think his legs have brought him here out of habit and his stomach out of hunger, but his mind is not here. His eyes have a faraway look and he sits like a dead man, unresponsive, his hands resting on the table beside his plate and as far as I see, he eats nothing. Burl is next to him and keeps glancing at him with a worried expression on his face. Once he catches me looking and gives a small smile and shake of the head.

I see Anton looking once or twice too. He knows what it is like. He has been there too, though maybe it wasn't the same. I think again about mother. She has lost her much loved husband. How do people cope? How long does it take?

Again, the routine we had established helps us to carry on through the difficult days after Miss Stepovich's death. Riley Allen seems to keep to his cabin most of the time, at least I never see him much, and when I do, his face is drawn. He has lost his boyish look and seems to have aged twenty years. His eyes are sightless and he even walks in a stiff unnatural manner so unlike his usual bouncy gait.

I decide to try and get into some sort of fitness again in preparation to taking up ballet as soon as I get back to Petrograd. I'm in poor physical shape having almost starved to death and then been fed but not exercised much. I have flesh in all the wrong places. I vow to spend some time each day doing some stretching and strengthening exercises if I can find enough space on the deck.

I discover that a good time is first thing in the morning. I begin getting up at six - thirty when it is barely light and doing an hour's work before breakfast. There is space on the poop deck near the brig.

Ivan has hardly bothered me since his dunking in the sea and I am past caring any more. I am more convinced than ever that ballet is to be my life and his ignorance is his loss.

I begin my warm up one morning as dawn is breaking. It is cool now that we are well into September but that suits me fine.

I hear some muttering and laughing and out of the corner of my eye a movement. Without stopping I turn to look. What seems like half the Japanese crew is assembled watching me and it is not an appreciative audience. I try to ignore them but two come out and stand in front of me and begin to mimic my moves but exaggerate them, making the others roar with laughter. If it was good humoured I could take it and join in, but it is not.

One by one others come forward, some to join in the grotesque parody of ballet and others to get right up close as if examining my movements in detail. Soon I am out of breath, not from dancing but from rage.

"Haven't you got anything to do?" I shout, but of course they don't understand and laugh the louder, now trying to mimic my language. I stop dancing and elbow my way through to the gangway leading down to the main deck. As I reach the steps, one of them puts out his foot. I don't see it coming and fall headfirst down to the deck below.

They cheer and that is as much as I can tolerate. Ignoring my bruised body, I fly up the steps and throw a punch at the nearest man, taking him completely by surprise. He loses his balance and falls backwards onto the deck, not, unfortunately down the steps.

For a moment the others step back out of my reach, then with a roar they surge forward and begin laying into me.

I am building up my muscles for ballet but they do just as well for fighting and the crew members don't get the better of me immediately. Eventually, of course, I am overpowered by sheer numbers and I hate to think what would have happened if Riley Allen hadn't come by to see what all the noise was about.

The crewmen scatter like ants and are gone in a moment. Once my adrenalin stops pumping round the pain hits me like a punch from a giant and I sit down on the top step and hug my bruised body.

"Are you all right, Nikolai?" asks Riley.

I manage to nod. He knows I'm not but I know what he means. No broken bones.

He stands over me waiting for me to recover enough to get back to my bunk and lie down.

"It's a good thing you were there," I say at last.

"I couldn't sleep," he says. "I was walking round the deck. I saw you up here earlier and watched you for a while. You have talent."

"Thank you."

"I'll report this to the captain."

I shake my head but he interrupts me before I can say anything. "You have a right to exercise unmolested," he says. "You should not have to put up with that, you had enough of it from Ivan."

I didn't realise he knew that.

I am excused lessons that day and one of the nurses gives me some ointment to put on my bruises. Word gets round about the fight and I find myself repeating the story and rather embellishing the way I knocked all the crew down and blackened a few eyes. Once I see Riley nearby and he is smiling. The first smile since Miss Stepovich's death, so that makes it all worthwhile.

By the time we enter the English channel Riley still has had no word from ARC headquarters in Washington about where we can go. We put in to Brest harbour, in France, but Riley is the only one to disembark. He is meeting with the American Red Cross official European Commissioner to try to sort something out.

After two days he comes back and reports to us. He refused to let us stay in a French camp while it was sorted out. We are to sail to the Baltic while the Commissioner tries to find a Baltic port which will accept us.

We are not home yet.

Another problem has arisen too. There are mines in the English channel. An English pilot comes on board to guide us through to the Kiel Canal and for several hours we jump at the slightest noise out of the ordinary, expecting to be blown to oblivion at any moment.

It didn't happen and on 2nd October 1920 we enter the Kiel Canal. This couldn't be more different from the Panama Canal. The land either side is very flat and green with lots of trees.

We four watch again from the rail. Anything is interesting after so long at sea.

"So how many men died building this canal?" I ask our walking encyclopaedia, Boris.

"None, as far as I know," he says, oblivious to the fact that I am teasing him. "It's one hundred kilometres long and was opened in 1895…"

There is no stopping him. You get the facts whether you want them or not, I think, but with affection. It's what friends are all about, tolerating their annoying habits. We have been together constantly for two and a half years and are still friends. I know they will be my friends for life.

We get up early the next morning and are at the rail as we leave Kiel and enter the Baltic Sea. Our chatter stops and we retreat into our own thoughts for some time.

"I can feel it," says Grigori at last. "We are nearing home. Petrograd is straight ahead. I don't see why we can't just sail there." He shades his eyes to look ahead into the rising sun and the open water as if Petrograd was about to come into view any moment. The wind is rising and blows his hair straight back and I can feel the movement beneath my feet increasing. The crew seems to be busy lashing things down.

"I think there's going to be a storm," I say.

"Why can't we go home?" Boris persists.

"We are going home," I say. "It's just that Riley wants to do it properly. We don't know what things are like in Petrograd now. He can't just dump us at the docks. Remember what Artur Popov's plans were? Riley can't risk the same thing happening."

"It's all political," says Grigori. "I'm going in. It's too cold here. You're right about the storm, Nikolai."

"Political," mumbles Boris. "Home is home."

I can't let it go. "Look, Riley says he wants to deliver us into the hands of our parents. You heard him. He wants to see it through to the end."

Boris shrugs and we all turn and stagger, buffeted by the rising wind, back inside.

That day the storm reaches hurricane proportions and all the following night we roll and pitch and huge waves crash onto the decks. We are confined to the holds and I, amongst many, suffer very bad seasickness. I have never felt so ill in my life except when we were starving in Koure, and to make things worse, the heaving causes stabbing pains from my bruised ribs.

The stench in the hold must be unbearable for those who are not affected by the motions of the ship and they are probably ill too on account of it. Two hundred people throwing up in a confined space for forty eight hours is indescribable.

Anton is not ill. He braves that stinking hold without complaint for the two days that the storm rages and he looks after me better than I deserve.

It's very difficult and dangerous to get to the toilets since they were constructed on the decks so we go in pairs, particularly when the little children need to go. Anton takes me and we stagger, clutching each other, from one hand hold to the other up the steps and through the hatch and into the howling wind. A rope has been rigged up and we cling to it, feeling the wind ready to scoop us up and toss us overboard like scraps of garbage.

It is during those times that fear begins to filter in and almost take precedence over the nausea. Can this small ship, overcrowded as she is, cope with such buffeting? Once there is a loud snap and then a tremendous flapping for a moment before whatever it was breaks free. There are other ominous sounds too, crashes and tearing noises, until we begin to wonder if the whole ship is disintegrating bit by bit.

On the third day the wind dies and the mountainous waves become hills. With relief, we begin to stagger up to the deck, weak from our ordeal. The sun is blinding as we emerge and stream on deck, only to find devastation.

The wind sails in front of the hatches have gone. So has the whole galley, which had been constructed on the starboard deck. The Red Cross staff cabins, also constructed on the deck, have collapsed, and I hope that they all escaped unharmed.

I tentatively take a deep breath of fresh air and notice that my ribs no longer hurt so much and the couple of days confinement to my bunk have nearly healed my other bruises. I begin to feel human again.

Grigori and Boris were both ill too and I catch sight of Ivan as he emerges from the hold. His face is ashen and catching me looking at him for once evokes no reaction.

"Where do you think we are?" asks Grigori, coming to stand beside me at the rail.

I shrug. "We still don't know where we're going and I don't suppose Riley was in contact with anyone during that storm."

"Maybe we didn't make any headway at all." He sounds despondent, almost defeated, and I turn to look at him.

"How do you feel?"

He doesn't answer the question but says, "I never want to go through that again. I don't care if I never see another ship."

I don't mention my bruised ribs.

Burl pushes through the crowd. "Is everyone all right?" There are nods. No-one feels much like talking yet.

"Nikolai? How are you?"

"I'm fine thank you," I say. "Are the staff all right?" I look across at their wrecked cabins.

He nods and smiles. "Got out in time. The galley's gone though. We don't know how we're going to manage to feed everyone."

When he leaves I say, "Don't spread this around, but we're really short on supplies and water. We need to dock somewhere soon."

Boris says nothing but stares out to sea.

Anton says, "We've been hungry before." I smile and pat him on the back. I am going to enjoy having such a brave, stoical brother. It crosses my mind that we will each, all eight hundred of us, have been affected by this ordeal and adventure we have been through. We will never know how much it shaped our personalities and outlook on life.

With nowhere to cook food apart from the ship's own small galley which is for the crew only, we exist on cold soup, canned meat and cheese. Water is to be strictly rationed. Riley says, since he has heard nothing from headquarters, we are going to try and dock at Helsingfors in Finland.

The entrance to Helsingfors harbour is through a narrow channel between two great pillars of rock. There are quite a number of ships in the harbour and we drop anchor offshore and watch as a Customs boat immediately speeds towards us.

Grigori grins as we watch. "They're not expecting us."

"Nor probably wanting us," says Boris.

The Customs men come on board and a while later we see Riley Allen accompany them down to the boat and head for the shore.

"Do your best, Riley," I say, although not loud enough for him to hear.

It is several hours before he comes back. We are sitting on deck eating our cold meal. He waves his hand for silence.

"I'm afraid I haven't any real news," he says. "We are negotiating with the Finnish government through our Red Cross official here but they are not keen to take us." He gives a small laugh to soften the implication that we are not wanted. "You must understand that Finland and your country are not exactly friends so they are not rushing to help. I have explained that we are very low on supplies, especially water, and that our only aim is to get you all safely back to your parents."

"I still don't see why we couldn't have gone straight to Petrograd," says Boris under his breath.

I nudge him, or rather poke him with my elbow. "They know best," I say, trying to keep my patience.

"Do they?"

Well, Riley must have used his charm and powers of persuasion again because the next day we are given permission to enter Finland. We are to stay in a sanatorium which was been built by the tsar for exclusive use by his family, back when Finland was a Russian province.

We leave Helsingfors and sail through the Gulf of Finland to a small port called Koivisto. Our voyage with the Yomei Maru has ended and as we disembark for the last time, carrying our few possessions, I look back at the ship. It is in a sorry state now. Some of the crew are watching and I know they must be relieved to see the back of us. I feel no malice towards them – well, not much. That experience on the poop deck is fading as new horizons open up ahead.

Trains take us part of the way to Halila and we have to walk the rest, but I, for one, don't mind. It is good to be ashore again. I am beginning to agree with Boris. I have seen enough of the sea for a while, if not a lifetime.

"I've been here before," says Grigori, "when it belonged to us. My grandfather had a dacha here when I was little. I remember the smell of the pine trees. In the garden there was a stream where we used to bathe."

"So it feels like home already?" I say.

"A little."

The air is cool and fresh and the smell of pine washes the remaining putrid air of the holds from our nostrils as we walk. More like home. Dark green pines tower on either side of the narrow road. The gravel crunches under our feet. A long long line of children winds towards its final destination. I can feel the atmosphere of hope all around.

It's a grand building, three stories high with a white dome and flagpole in the centre of the main part. On either side are two more wings making three sides of a square. The approach is by a long straight drive so that you can admire the house long before you reach it.

It's by far the best place we have stayed at in our long journey, clean and well maintained and we fall into the rooms and claim our beds with joy.

During the first evening meal Riley promises to keep us informed as to what is happening. Another man has joined him. A square-jawed fine-looking man with deep blue eyes and dark curly hair. He's the man who is helping Riley, the ARC commissioner to the Baltic, Edward Ryan.

"Let me make it clear what our plans are," goes on Riley. "We have a list of the last known addresses of your parents. We shall send that list to the Parents' Committee in Petrograd asking your parents to write to you agreeing to your return. There is no communication between Finland and Russia so we have arranged to send the letters via Estonia."

"So we just wait," shouts Karl.

"You wait," says Riley.

It's the waiting that is so difficult. The routine, as usual, keeps us busy but the anticipation, the way heads go up expectantly every time one of the Red Cross staff comes into a room – that is hard. We are all restless, wanting to move on.

Then one day it happens.

After tea we are told to assemble in the main hall. The din of chatter stops the instant Riley Allen comes into the room. My heart is pounding so loudly I think everyone could hear it. Anton and I exchange hopeful smiles.

Riley is carrying a sack which he places on a table, then he turns to speak to us.

"Letters from your parents have arrived," he says. There is a collective gasp and shuffling of feet restless to be on their way.

"Not everyone has a letter yet," he says. "About two hundred came today. Don't despair if your name isn't called out. It may be your turn next time." He reaches into the sack and pulls out a sheaf of letters. Then he begins to call out names.

There are tears and little screams of joy as children rush forward to take their letter and find a private place to read it.

Anton and I are not amongst them but Grigori has his and his wide grin says it all. His eyes glisten with tears as he waves the letter in the air. He cannot speak.

No-one else we know well is in this first lot. These people are to be taken to the border, fifteen miles away, on November 10th, where they will be officially handed over to our Russian authorities.

Anton is clearly disappointed, as am I. "Maybe next time," I say. But what if something has happened to mother? It is such a long time since we had any news. The Red Cross people told us how bad things still are in Petrograd but a little doubt creeps into my mind. Is it as bad as they say? I know they are very much against our Communist government so perhaps they are trying to make it sound worse than it is. Surely the idea is to improve things for people after the poverty under the tsars.

A farewell party is planned for the evening before the departure of those children who have received letters. I look at their faces and envy them.

"We are lucky," says Anton, stuffing a piece of cake into his mouth.

"Why?" I ask, feeling guilty at my thoughts.

"We nearly starved to death and now we have too much to eat."

Isn't that just like my brother? I don't tell him that it might not always be the case.

The next morning the whole Colony stands outside the building to say goodbye to those lucky ones. I find myself hugging people I have never met before, and exchanging addresses. Then they detach themselves from the rest of us and we watch the line of children walk down the drive with Riley and an assistant at their head. We watch until they are out of sight and then turn slowly and go back inside. We feel bereft, as if a limb has been torn away. Suddenly I notice how cold it is and shiver. Winter comes suddenly in this part of the world.

Riley and his assistant arrive back late that afternoon and everyone wants to know every detail of the handover. He nods, understanding as always. The sadness in his eyes is still there.

"The border is just a small river," he says. "Not much more than a stream really. It's called the Little Black River. The only crossing is a rickety wooden bridge."

A platoon of Russian soldiers had been waiting for them and Riley had insisted that each child call out their number as they crossed so that the officer in charge could check off their name.

My number will be emblazoned on my heart forever, I think.

Some of the parents had made the journey to the border and others were waiting at Petrograd railway station.

"It was so hard to see them go after all this time," says Riley, quietly. "I shall miss you all."

Boris is in the next batch and Alexei and Karl in the one after that. Slowly our numbers are dwindling and it is strange not to be part of such a big group any more. The atmosphere in Halila becomes more and more depressing as each lot of children leave. Winter is well and truly upon us and there is over a metre of snow outside. It is so cold that we hardly ever go outside and I spend a lot of time gazing out of the frosted windows. I have almost stopped doing any exercises too.

The building is beginning to sound hollow as it empties and now you can find a whole room to yourself – ideal for my practice, but I can feel the spirit and joy of dancing draining away. Anton notices and gives me such a talking to that I decide to resume, if just to please him.

Late one afternoon I go looking for an empty room and I hear weeping. Pushing open the door I see Tatiana crouching in a corner, her face in her hands.

I go in and quietly close the door. If she hears me she doesn't look up.

"Tatiana."

The sobs stop and she raises her head a little.

"Oh, it's you, Nikolai," she says in a muffled voice, and then wipes her eyes on her sleeve with one arm as she reaches into her pocket for a handkerchief.

"Our turn will come," I say, sitting down on the floor in front of her. "There are still a lot of us left who haven't had a letter yet." I speak with more conviction than I feel. I wonder what will happen to any of us who never receive a letter.

She shakes her head. "It's not that," she says, and gives a small laugh. "My parents are too busy to write back in a hurry. There are both doctors remember. I think I was a mistake. I just get in the way."

I know the pointlessness of arguing.

"So why are you crying?" I hear myself say, as if that isn't enough reason.

"It's Burl."

I wonder if I've heard right. "Burl?"

"He's seeing a lot of another girl."

Then I remember. She likes Burl. She is in love with Burl. She told me that way back in New York.

"But…' I can't believe this but I don't want to trivialise it. 'Did he ever say…?" I begin again.

She furiously blows her nose and looks up at me with swollen eyes. "You wouldn't understand. No, he never said… anything, but I hoped. I thought he liked me. I can't imagine life without him." A fresh spate of sobs.

I stand up. "Tatiana."

She looks up at the sudden harshness of my voice.

"I can't believe this is you. You are the most mature, practical, intelligent girl I know – I thought that from the first moment I met you when you spoke at the meeting in Koure, yet here you are snivelling over a man who is too old for you, who is American and who obviously is not in love with you."

I see her eyes darken with anger so I beat her to it. "You may think your parents don't care but I'm sure they wouldn't want you to go and live in America anyway. Could you honestly see yourself leaving Russia and everything you know? He may already have a girlfriend over there anyway."

"He would have said."

"Why would he? His job is to look after us and see us safely home. Of course he is nice to everyone, that's Burl. He's funny and kind and friendly. You have your future ahead and that future is in Russia, besides, I want you to come and see me perform when I'm famous."

She smiles then, and I do too, reaching down to help her to her feet.

"You'll still be friends with me even when you're famous?" she asks.

I laugh again. "Of course. Now leave me alone, I have my practice to do."

Cheering Tatiana up actually has the effect of cheering me up too and I begin my exercises with renewed vigour and enthusiasm.

That night one of the girls goes missing.

Chapter 18

I don't know her although when she is described to me I remember seeing her around. Her name is Maria, she is only seven and had become very upset at having had no letter yet from her parents. A search party is formed and I volunteer to join. We are loaned extra clothes and pack newspaper into our shoes. It is the middle of December and the sun barely rises above the horizon at this time of year. We only have six hours of daylight.

We set off down the drive with Burl leading. It's logical that she would stick to the road and not stray off into the forest. It's bitterly cold but luckily there is no wind. No-one could last long in these conditions and we have to find her before nightfall. We have no lamps and she would not survive the night.

We find her huddled under a tree by the side of the road about three miles from the house. She's barely conscious and so cold that it takes a time for her to stand up straight from her curled position. Burl has brought a flask of hot tea which is barely warm now but it seems to revive her enough to hoist her onto Burl's back for the journey home.

When she has thawed out in front of the fire, Riley asks her gently why she ran away.

"Because," she says in a whisper that we all strain to hear, "I can't go home with everyone else."

"Why not?" asks Riley.

Maria looks up at him briefly and then down at the floor, as if ashamed.

"I can't remember what my mother looks like."

Riley hugs her to him. "You will know her when you see her," he says. "And she will know you too. You wait and see."

"It's funny," says Anton later. "I can hardly remember what mother looks like either but I can remember father clearly."

It's the first time he's mentioned father so it seems to me that a sort of healing process has begun.

New Year comes and goes and we try hard to celebrate. From nearly eight hundred children there are only ninety left. Riley and the Red Cross staff are determined that we shall have Christmas though, and he confides that he is going to play Santa Claus to the younger ones.

"That role suits you," I say, and he raises his eyebrows enquiringly. "What, you mean I'm overweight?"

I laugh and shake my head. He certainly isn't that. "You remember in Koure it was Christmas Eve when you rescued us."

"So it was," he says. "So it was."

He knows, and all we older ones know, that this will be our last Christmas. Last legal one anyway. For some reason it has now been banned in Russia, as have all religious festivals. When Anton asks why, Riley says that Communism and Religion don't go together. But, he says, no-one can outlaw what we believe in our hearts.

On January 13th Tatiana receives a letter from her parents and is all smiles. We say goodbye and promise to keep in touch.

On January 26th Anton and I have a letter from mother. She is well. She is overjoyed that we are safe and she is counting the hours until she sees us.

Ours is the final batch of letters. Only one person never receives one.

Ivan.

That night he disappears and it is assumed that he headed for the border and crossed over alone – if he survived the night at sub zero temperatures.

The Little Black River is just that. Very insignificant in itself yet marking a very important boundary. The bridge over it is as Riley described, a sort of rope bridge with wooden slats. A larger bridge nearby has been destroyed and all that is left are a few thick timber struts now covered in snow.

The soldier in the middle of the bridge looks cold and bored and is probably looking forward to an end to this tedious trek back and forth escorting groups of children from one side to the other.

This time there are only forty-five of us so it doesn't take long. Anton hugs Riley and I shake his hand and thank him for everything. He clings to our hands and is too choked up to speak. At last he manages, 'Good luck. Keep in touch.'

I nod and Anton and I step onto the bridge, gripping the rope hand holds as it sways.

"Twenty-two," I say for the last time.

As we reach the other side I stop to look back. Riley is already walking away, his shoulders hunched, whether against the cold or from sadness I don't know. Knowing Riley, I'd guess the latter. He is probably oblivious to the cold.

I look ahead again and step determinedly onto Russian soil.

Several parents are there and I scan the faces. None of them looks like mother. I feel a slight disappointment but it *is* the middle of winter. She will be at Petrograd station for sure.

"Nikolai? Anton?"

I look up. A woman stands in front of us. Anton rushes and hugs her but I just stare at her face. She is gaunt and pale and has aged twenty years in the two and a half years since we last saw her. Her hair is thin and pulled back to a knot behind her neck. Wisps of it have escaped and drift about her face.

My thoughts must show in my face as usual because she gives me a wan smile and a small nod of the head. Then she enfolds me in her arms and the three of us turn as one to make our way to the waiting sleighs.

Chapter 19

26 Waimea Road
Oahu
Hawaii
16th February 1922

Dear Nikolai,

Many thanks for your welcome letter. I, too, cannot believe that already a year has passed since the end of our great trip together. I think of it often, and with a certain nostalgia. There were many problems – more than you young people ever knew, but it was an experience I shall never forget. There were good times and bad, weren't there?

I have settled back into my job as editor of the Honolulu Star Bulletin. It seems a bit tame after our adventures.

We are enjoying a mild winter so think of us in the sunshine!

Congratulations on your dancing achievement! I told you you had talent. Work hard. Maybe we shall see you performing here some day, or in Los Angeles or San Francisco perhaps? I would make a special trip over there to see you.

The photo you sent of yourself playing the lead role in *Petrushka* sits on my desk and I'm looking at it as I write.

I'm glad to hear that Anton is doing well at school too. Please give him my regards, and your mother too, although I never met her.

You have no need to apologise for your English, Nikolai. It is very good – far better than my Russian (I don't have much chance to practice here). So you have read *Huckleberry Finn*? Well done. I hope you enjoyed it.

I would love to see your country sometime, and thank you for your invitation. I'm told that Petrograd is a beautiful city.

Yes, I do hear from some of the others from the Colony from time to time. It's wonderful that we can keep in touch. If I never have any children of my own I shall always think of you all as mine. All eight hundred of you!

Yours,
Riley Allen.

Made in the USA
Monee, IL
07 May 2023

33281511R00100